Red Oleanders

A Drama in One Act

Rabindranath Tagore

Foreword by
Mohit K. Ray

Introduction by
Rama Kundu

PEACOCK BOOKS

FOREWORD

We are happy to place in the hands of our scholars and lovers of Tagore, all over the world, a new edition of *Red Oleanders* (1925, Tagore's own translation of his Bengali play *Raktakarabī* (published in 1924), with a comprehensive critical introduction by Professor Rama Kundu, by way of paying our homage to Tagore on the auspicious occasion of the year-long celebrations of the 150th birth anniversary of the poet. (1861-1941).

Raktakarabī belongs to the symbolic phase (1922-1932) of Tagore's experimentations with the dramatic form. The themes—materialism versus humanism, industry versus agriculture, possessive greed versus selfless love, etc.—are all superbly integrated into the symbolic structure of the play, which is a powerful dramatic evocation of the evils of mindless industrialism, and celebrates the perennial values of love, life and nature. In its symbolic suggestions and dramatic situations, luminous diction and lyrical resonance, the play is a literary *tour de force* and is comparable with any great play of the world.

In her brilliant and comprehensive Introduction, Rama Kundu touches on all the major aspects of the play, its genesis and themes, ideas and symbols, images and metaphors, historical, social and political contexts, characters and situations, songs and dances, the meaning and the music, and intertextual parallels, leaving virtually nothing *en route.*

I am sure, that the Introduction, while adding to the understanding and enjoyment of the play, will also be immensely useful to all Tagore scholars.

Mohit K. Ray
(Chief Editor)
Atlantic Publishers and Distributors (P) Ltd.

CONTENTS

INTRODUCTION

If you searched for meanings under the petals of the red oleander that would lead to disaster.

['Preface', Rabindranath Tagore]

Raktakarabī (1924)/*Red Oleanders* (1925) is one of Tagore's best plays; and understandably 'meanings' have been sought 'under the petals', in spite of the author's admonition, by countless readers, theatre-goers, performers/producers, and literary critics.

Anyway, as each of Tagore's works calls back and forth to the other works in his great oeuvre, this play too has to be seen in the total perspective in order to get at the 'meaning'. What indeed Tagore did not turn his myriad mind upon? If we consider just the plays, even that can prove a challenging job, in view of the variety and fecundity involved. The plays have been grouped in various arrangements among which the one made by Pramathanath Bishi—a former resident pupil at the *ashram* of Shantiniketan during Tagore's time, and subsequently an eminent Tagore scholar—has been generally accepted as the standard grouping.

According to Bishi, Tagore's plays may be classified into the following eight categories: (1) musical drama, (2) verse drama, (3) romantic tragedy, (4) play of ideas/symbolic drama, (5) social plays, (6) comedy, (7) seasonal plays, and (8) dance drama. Bishi places *Raktakarabī* (*Red Oleanders*) in the fourth category.

Furthermore, Pramathanath Bishi classifies Rabindranath's 'plays of ideas'/'symbolic drama' into three phases: the first phase is represented by *Prakṛtir Pratiśodh*; the second phase includes *Śāradotsav*, *Acalāyatan*, *Rājā* and *Dākghar*; whereas the third phase comprises *Fālguṇī*, *Muktadhārā*, *Raktakarabī* (*Red Oleanders*), *Rather Raśi*, *Tāser Deś*, and *Kabir Dīkṣā*.

Play of Ideas and Symbols

This genre is Tagore's unique contribution to Bengali drama; this had been his own innovation on the Bengali stage, which has been subsequently pursued by very few Bengali dramatists indeed, as Upendranath Bhattacharya points out.

Red Oleanders is a play more oriented in ideas than action. It belongs to the group of Tagore's plays which elaborately draw upon myths, allegories, signs, symbols, while dealing with some major problems/predicaments of human life and situation. The dominance of ideas marks out this group from his other plays, in which the story element or action takes priority; even when a story is there it is the idea which informs and rules the story.

Genesis

Like all masterpieces the process of the creation of *Raktakarabī* (*Red Oleanders*) had started much earlier, and at various turns various elements had entered into the making, and took shape through long years of silent nurturing.

In course of Tagore's trip to Europe in 1912, and return after a long spell abroad, his initial fascination with modern Europe was got over; the disillusionment was further reinforced by a deep anxiety about an impending 'crisis of civilization', which he thought, would overcome mankind as a consequence of its blind mechanical pursuit of material wealth and power. Again, this was the period that coincided with his winning the Nobel award which was followed by many a trip abroad; the publicity attending the award also brought in its train the imposed/attributed image of the spiritual spokesman and messenger of India for the war-torn world; by this time that the First World War came to a close.

In the meantime, Shantiniketan which had been started in December 1901, had already expanded considerably, thereby thrusting more and more wearying responsibilities upon the poet; lack of money had become chronic botheration, along with various efforts taken to tide over the crises. Alongside the demands made upon him by the institution, there were demands of the country and the world—and all this piled upon one another, had been disturbing and eating into his leisure, time and energy. All the time the urge to write was pressing him inside. There was also no end to hostility within the country and abroad. Friends were few; surrounded by dull devotees who looked up to him as the '*gurudev*', and whom he could neither reject nor accept altogether.

It was around this time that a little girl drifted into his life. Her name was Ranu. She came like a breath of fresh wind amidst the suffocating climate around. Her frequent visits to Shantiniketan coincided with the joining of Elmherst in the work of Sriniketan and his delightful vibrant presence.

These various events of personal life were entering the crucible of imagination, and getting metamorphosed there under the wonderful chemistry of creativity, which ultimately took shape in the play *Raktakarabī*.

In a poem of Tagore, titled 'Vijayee' (The Victorious) published in the journal *Prabāsī* in 1918, and later included in the anthology of poems, *Pūrabī*, one can trace some of the ideas of the play in an embryonic form.

Raktakarabī and *Red Oleanders*

Tagore's translation of the play

It may seem interesting that the English version of the play came out before the original Bengali version was published in book form. *Red Oleanders*, the author's own translation of his *Raktakarabī*, was published in 1925, and the Bengali book was published in 1926, although it had come out in the journal *Prabāsī* in autumn 1924.

Unlike Tagore's other auto-translations, a few departures or transformations can be noted from the original in the translation. Certain passages in some of the dialogues have been omitted or shortened. For instance, Nandini's impassioned interrogation of the system in which the King is kept off behind a net becomes a succinct cool composed sharp query in the English version:

> Then again, you hide your king behind a wall of netting. Is it for fear of people finding out that he's a man? (4)

The dialogue between Fagulal and Chandra about the close proximity of tavern, armory and temples in the Yakshapuri has been omitted. On the other hand, some completely new speeches have been inserted on occasions: for instance, Fagulal tells Chandra in a tone of annoyance which only fails to hide his despair: "Don't worry me, Chandra. A thousand times over have I told you that in these parts there are high roads to the market, to the burning ground, to the scaffold—everywhere except to the homeland" (15).

On one occasion the order of speeches in a dialogue between Nandini and the 'voice' has been reversed.

Raktakarabī, like many a play of Tagore, touches the poetic heights, and perhaps it is only natural that often in the translation we miss the pulsation of the original rhythm, the sweet resonance of music, the sharpness of images; the language too seems to have been shorn of much of the fascinating charm of the original.

When it is closely following the original, we find the author using additional words/phrases in order to come up close behind the source. As a result, the simple sentences too occasionally turn complex in the English rendering.

Also some music has been done away with. For instance, in response to Nandini's query why did Bishu leave her silently in the past, Bishu sings a wonderful, deeply moving song in *Raktakarabī*. In *Red Oleander* that song is not presented; instead some lines of the song have been transferred into Bishu's speech: "My boat was tied to the bank; the rope snapped; the wind drove it into the trackless unknown" (21).

In his song Bishu addresses Nandini as 'O waker of my grief!' (21); the musical effect of *ogo dukha-jāgāniā* in Bengali is altogether missing in the English version; the soft endearing intimate colloquial address, along with its melody, loses its charm and evocation in the literally correct translation.

The choric song recurring through the play *Raktakarabī* with remarkable aesthetic effect has been retained in the

English version. But the author has made a slight change from the source; in the Bengali version it is '*Pauş*', meaning winter (December-January), i.e. the traditional harvesting season of Bengal; but in translation, perhaps in keeping with the empirical/climatological context of the TL (Target Language) the author has made it 'Autumn', which is further specified accurately as 'September', which marks the West's season of harvesting and 'mellow fruitfulness'.

Time and Place

Both the space and time have been used paradigmatically, according to the requirement of the symbolic play, and not in the manner of a realistic play.

(a) *Time*

(i) The Diurnal backdrop

Mention has been made of various segments of time, from morning to sunset; but the spectator, under the spell of the play, tends to forget how many days the action is spread over, and what particular era of human history constitutes the location.

Anyway, what is the exact time-frame of the play? Is it just one day? We come to know early that this is a holiday on the occasion of Flag-worship, and Weapon-worship. Yet Bishu stops Nandini's joyous outpour, saying, "let me go to my work". And Nandini implores: "Run away, Kishor, go back to your work, quick! You'll be late again" (3). On a further consideration it seems that perhaps this is not the event of any particular day; many events of many days have been telescoped into the space of one day,—like Solzhenitsyn's *One Day in the Life of Ivan Denisovich*, or like the one week epitomizing the endless time in Kafka's *Castle*.

The opening of the play gives the impression of some morning hour—as suggested by little touches like gathering flower, or stitching a garland of flowers. The harvest song too, sung in that morning, denotes signs of the hour. The mellow morning light of autumn is, as it were, subsumed in the charming golden hue of the ripe corn. Later, as Nandini reports to Bishu about the song she heard in the 'morning', apparently the day has advanced meanwhile. Towards the end it is already evening coming down: 'the play of the field is ended now, and the field-master is taking the ripe corn home' (253).

(ii) Seasonal backdrop

The immediate seasonal backdrop is autumn (though winter in the Bengali version) that provides the backdrop. In the original version the seasonal backdrop is mid-winter, the time for shearing the corn; with the imminent festival of '*Nabānna*', a popular harvesting ritual of rural India, knocking at the door. Again, the winter is also congenial for digging work. Thus the season itself contains the seed of conflict between the principles of cultivation and mining.

Here one must take note of the fact that winter in Eastern India is not the winter of Europe; the connotations are completely different. However, in the English version the poet changes it to 'Autumn'; possibly because in Europe autumn is the harvesting time and winter is associated with the idea of death and hardship, barren landscape, bleak sky, though in India it is the beautiful season of bright pleasant days, flagged off by the harvesting rituals. Incidentally, autumn also happened to be Tagore's favorite season which signified for him nature's prosperity, benediction and fulfillment.

The season in the play foregrounds the counterpoints—harvesting and digging; the call for the delightful festival of the new crop, and the horrifying drunken carnival of *Dhwajāpujā* or Flag-worship. On occasions the song of shearing the crop in the distant cornfields wafts in through the horrible noise of the town. Unlike Tagore's *Śāradotsav* and *Post-office*, the two plays preceding *Red Oleanders*, which show a harmony between the human mood and the seasonal mood, here the disharmony is apparent. In the distant cornfields the season represents the contrastive light and sound to those of the human world in the town; the season has sprinkled gold in abandon through its golden sunlight upon golden cornears in contrast to the dark innards of the earth's bowel with its dead gold. It sends its joyous sun-burnt music which is in contrast to the hideous roar of the machine.

(b) *Place*

Whereas the Yaksha Town takes the foreground as the dramatic space, at the backdrop—far behind though—there is the cornfield with ripe corn, which is evoked rather than presented.

(i) Yaksha town

Tagore writes: "like Swarnalanka, the locale of my *Pālā*, where the events take place, has a name; to the poet's cognition it is Yakshapuri" (trans. present author). The name of the place suggests a mythical or legendary dimension. Yaksha is another name for Kuber, the deity of wealth in the extended Hindu pantheon; but unlike Lakshmi, who is also a deity of wealth, Kuber does not have either grace, or beauty, or benediction; he is a lesser god in the pantheon, who is most wealthy yet lacking in other godly attributes.

The description/account of Yaksha Town that we find in the play carries resemblance to (1) a mining area, (2) a modern industrial city, and (3) a place under the rule of some autocratic oppressive government.

The author says, "It is possible that there should be controversy among cartographers about the exact location of the place. But everybody knows it is called by the name Yakshapuri. Scholars would say, Oh, the legendary Yakshapuri! Isn't it the place of Kuber, with the golden throne? But this play is neither legend nor allegory". The author explains, "The place referred to, contains the treasure of Yaksha kept entombed under the earth" (*Nāṭyaparicay*; my translation).

Yakshapuri represents such a society where there has been a lack of life, a lack of piety which becomes apparent in its assault upon life, love, *joie de vivre*, beauty. Here life is repressed by the ignominy of forced labour, oppression, exploitation, by the denial of light and pure joy of the sunlit cornfield; here life is besotted by stale vulgar mirth of inebriation; here life is crippled and perverted by fear and the worship of weapons; it is a death-in-life existence.

Yakshapuri has been presented as a 'city of eclipse' where people 'in their drunken fury…tear the earth's veils to pieces'

(6). Even holidays here are not like those back at home; because here it is the holiday of 'caged birds', and 'more of a nuisance than work'.

The place makes one insensitive to beauty. Gokul, who is suspicious by nature, cannot trust Nandini, and is particularly suspicious of her beauty; he would opt for features that are 'plain enough to understand'. Bishu sadly replies: "I know the atmosphere of this place breeds contempt for beauty. There must be beauty even in hell; but nobody there can understand it, that's their cruelest punishment" (12).

Once somebody chances to drift or step into the place there is no exit route. The road to freedom in the lap of nature is closed for ever. It is a strange labyrinth from which none can escape. Bishu had once tried to go home: "And then I found that, as soon as one enters the maw of Yaksha Town, its jaws shut fast, and the one road that remains open leads withinwards" (14); eventually a time comes when even the longing to escape has died. "Your Governor has closed the way as well as the will to return" (14). The vast 'prison' allows 'no open sky, no leisure' for its prisoners; and they have no access to pure joy, but only to the polluted drink of the prison (13). Coming here, the men 'go to the dogs' while the women wither up, as the simple charms of life recede for ever.

In contrast to the distant sunlit cornfields, Yakshapuri is a dark, blind, blinding hell of a place. As Chandra appeals to the Governor for leave to go home, she pleads in vain: "Don't you see that your men here work all day in the dark, and in the evening steep themselves in the denser dark of drunkenness?" (16). Such sharp touches seem to evoke the acute Zolaesque realism depicting the shabby seediness of slum life forced upon the industrial labor. Nandini mentions the place as 'this closed fort' (20) in which only 'a bit of sky' has survived between Bishu and herself. Bishu's reply to Nandini brings out the regimentation enforced by the system of the place: "Ever since coming to Yaksha Town the sky has dropped out of my life. I felt as if they had pounded me in the same mortar with all the fractions of men here, and rolled us into a solid lump" (20). This is like 'one day in the life of Ivan Denisovich' inside the inescapable jaws of the 'Gulag', i.e. Soviet concentration camps, as has been recorded by Alexander Solzhenitsyn in his Nobel-winning play.

Yakshapuri represents more of a system than any actual place, and the system thrives on fear. Nandini tells the King without mincing her words: "The people here trade on frightening others. That's why they have put you behind a network and dressed you fantastically" (26-27). It is the 'stone walls around' her that Nandini seeks to defy when she challenges the king, "Your stone walls will also fall away from around me today…" (25). But the system of the place allows no protest; you can at best just survive,—a kind of death-in-life, 'a dead and alive existence' (34); and that too on the condition of abject servility. No show of heroics would be tolerated for a moment. Gajju's humiliation is a case in point. Gajju, the once fearless wrestler is made to realize, "They only feel safe when they rob the whole world of strength" (35).

Even the sound of this place is anti-music, and horrifying.

Eventually the system breaks down,—not under attack from outside, but from internal disintegration, as an exploitative oppressive society may eventually crumble and collapse with rebellious upsurge from within itself. However, if we try to fit the play tightly into this, or any other, abstract frame, that would be an over-simplification. Rabindranath had said, the Yaksha Town existed across ages and places in the world in various forms, and at various layers. It may be compared, in this regard, to Kafka's 'Castle', which is located in no definite time-frame or spatial geography to particularize the setting, so that it becomes the story of all places in all times. It could indeed stand for any place in the modern times where the individual man/woman has been reduced to helplessness and subjected to indignity, humiliation, annihilation by the power-establishment controlling all. The wrestler, after having been 'altogether hollowed out', knows by his own terrible ordeal "These demons know the magic art of sucking away not only strength but hope" (35).

Thus Yakshapuri can be connected with the literary dystopias that were yet to come out; Koestler's 'Dark Noon', Solzhenitsyn's 'Gulag', George Orwell's 'Oceania', for instance, —the memorable semiotics of the unbearable humiliation that can be thrust upon common men in their everyday life. It is also symptomatic of the same pervasive mistrust generated by the stifling atmosphere of the place. Phagulal, who has always trusted Nandini in spite of the situation, is shaken when Bishu disappears, and sadly admits: "Every person suspects every other person in this cursed place" (45).

The perpetrators of oppression throw up a robot-like posture of mechanical operation. The Governor's assumption of dreadful impersonality behind the affairs of the place stuns Nandini, who exclaims: "Dear me, what an awful place! You are not men, and those you drive are not men, either,—you are winds and they are clouds!" (37). Appropriately, here persons are not recognized as individuals, but identified as abstract numbers.

Some factual details are made quite realistic; for instance the labors' twelve-hour day (just two years prior to the publication of the play the working hours were reduced from twelve to eleven); or the impossibility of leaving the job and go home; not only for the slaves, but also for the contract labor in many colonies, (say in the tea-gardens in our country it was valid till 1925,) there was no scope for leaving the job or place; that would be considered violation of contract and punishable with imprisonment or fine. The system is coming back in the form of SEZ today in parts of Asia and the world. So when Bishu says, 'Alas, the road is closed', this is no poetry but harsh reality. Yaksha Town is again emerging as a most adequate prevision of our own times, when "we have become trapped in an inescapable complicated situation because of our avarice for machine-generated prosperity" (Mitra 35; my translation); since the 1960s it has been apparent that, we have damaged and are doing further damage to the ozone layer; poisoned the water, the fish, the milk, vegetables, meat everything by our application of chemical fertilizer and pesticide; that by rending the earth's bosom we have pulled up with our booty "the curse of its dark demon, blind and hard, cruel and envious" (8).

Action

(i) Structure of action: The three phases

Shambhu Mitra, who had staged the play with spectacular success, traced three *Caraṇ*'s (parts/phases) within the continuous pace of the text. The first phase, as identified by Mitra, seems to be a kind of introduction. The end of the first dialog between Nandini and the King marks the end of the first phase, during which the spectator has been introduced to Yaksha Town, its creator, and its potential destructor; the spectator also gets a feel of some imminent storm gathering somewhere in the invisible horizon. We feel that there is some deep embedded conflict in the realm of its thought, its ideology.

During the second phase we get an even more elaborate picture of the Town society, and get hints that the conflict exists at the social level as well. When Nandini leaves with Bishu, following her second conversation with the 'Voice' behind the net, the second phase comes to its close. The transition from the second phase to the third is made poignant with a 'song of waiting', which quivers with sadness and premonition of the moment.

Then suddenly the third phase starts with a bang, as Governor declares harshly and loudly, "No, we cannot…allow Ranjan to enter this parish" (29). With this the pace of events quickens, rapidly heading towards the catastrophe. The conflicts we have already seen in the previous phases now head for crisis.

(ii) The conflict

It can be said, albeit simplistically, that Tagore here brings out the clash between agriculture-oriented civilization and accumulative industrial civilization, or to use his own words, between the *Karşaṇjībī* and *Ākarşaṇjībī* (tillers and diggers). It must be remembered however that the play was not written with the deliberate and exclusive intention to bring out the clash between *Karşaṇjībī* and *Ākarşaṇjībī*, and announce victory for any of the sides. That would be a rather simplistic and reductive view of the play. And, though this is a problem of a comparatively modern era, Tagore himself would not subscribe to the view that there was any such thing as a 'modern problem', as all major problems of man were held by him as perennial. In order to highlight the perenniality of the problem he has invited us to look back to the realms of the great Indian epic, *The Rāmāyaṇa.*

The Rāmāyaṇa and *Red Oleander:* Some Common Paradigms

(i) The Rāmāyaṇa: An Allegory

Tagore thought that in the clash between Rama and Ravana, the hero and anti-hero in the *Rāmāyaṇa*, the very same conflict had been envisioned by the poet Valmiki. He further claimed the same problem had been addressed by both the ancient poet and the modern playwright, i.e. Tagore himself.

The Rāmāyaṇa itself, Tagore thought, could be considered an elaborate allegory, especially when considered in the light of the two names: "Rama and Ravana, the two names carry two contrastive suggestions; Rama means comfort, peace; Ravana means noise, disturbance. One denoted the grace and sweetness of the new twig, the murmur of the foliage; the other the horrible grating of the monstrous chariot upon the concrete road." (Preface to *Raktakarabī*; my translation)

In another essay written way back in 1816 (*Bhāratbarṣer Itihāser Dhārā* [The course of India's History]) we find Tagore's discourse on the *Rāmāyaṇa* anticipating the view, expressed so many years later in his preface to the play, i.e. connecting Rama with agricultural civilization. It is from this angle that even the episodes of an earlier phase of Rama's life seem to fall in a pattern to the poet's perception. In his perception Rama emerges as the cult hero of an agrarian civilization. So he is symbolically the husband of 'Sita', a name which also means the furrow opened up before the plough; furthermore, Rama releases Ahalya from the curse of remaining a piece of stone by the roadside. 'Ahalya', again, is a name associated with agriculture; 'ahalya' means not ploughable. Tagore's interpretation is that the land which had been left aside by earlier sages as fallow rocky terrain, was brought under cultivation and thereby rejuvenated to life through the agricultural intervention of Rama.

Tagore thus offered an allegorical reading of the epic in which he seemed to have found a paradigmatic rendering of a historical phenomenon—the Aryans' eventual acceptance of the agricultural ways, and a subsequent battle between the community of growers/tillers of the earth with the community of diggers/plunderers of the earth, in which ultimately the former wins over the latter. Similar views are reiterated later (1930) in his, *Jāvāyātrīr Patra* (Letter of the voyager to Java).

(ii) Precursor and Ephebe

According to Pramathanath Bishi, Tagore had cast *Red Oleanders* as far as possible on the paradigm of the *Rāmāyaṇa.* Rabindranath himself has left an observation in this regard which can be considered almost a page taken from Harold Bloom, albeit a much later arrival in this world. Anticipating a typical Bloom-ian tone of delightful mock-insinuation Tagore, as 'ephebe', argues, towards 'exposing' the 'precursor' poet Valmiki's subtle 'appropriation' of an issue of a much later time in his ancient epic. With the ephebe's anxiety to get over the influence of the 'precursor', he writes:

> I shall give another instance to show how the great poet managed to sneak into the treasury house of the future by using his magic cutter of imaginative vision, and with what fine skill grabbed the property of future.
>
> There is a strong conflict between two categories of civilization,—*Karṣaṇjībī* (growers) and *Ākarṣaṇjībī* (plunderers). I often discuss this with my friends. This *Kaliyug* has been unceasingly ruining the villages by means of drawing people from the work of cultivation and engaging them to the work of plunder. Besides, hunger and thirst, the envy and jealousy, the luxury and illusions/confusions of the exploitative civilization are precisely like those of the highly skilled rakshasas. This observation of mine has been secretly appropriated by the poet into his bag of symbols; it becomes apparent to any attentive reader. Ravana, with the ten faces, the ruler of the golden realm, abducts

> Sita, the beloved darling of Ramachandra, with complexion like the fresh green grass; is it a tale of the ancient times, or of our own time? Is it the experience of a sage of the *Tretāyug*, or rightfully that of a poet of the *Kaliyug*, like me? Or had the proprietors of gold mines already coerced the peasants so long ago, the peasants who used to indulge in the luxury of the fresh green grassy land? (my translation)

Tagore had further applied the idea to the life of Valmiki himself. He wrote in the same context:

> Initially Ratnakar was a bandit. Eventually he had given up the vocation and become a devotee of Rama. The implication is that he overcame the lure of plundering as profession and had his initiation in the expertise of cultivation, and it was only then that he got the blessing of the beautiful, and music resonated through his lyre. This theory had touched the minds of people even in those days. As the former bandit emerged as poet, the message of the triumph of forest-dwellers over the golden Lanka resounded so powerfully through his voice. (my translation)

Indeed, this was an idea which had been stirring in the poet's mind since decades. And he has left quite a few observations in this regard.

In his prologue to the play Tagore referred to the *Rāmāyaṇa* in such words as would seem an anticipation of Harold Bloom—that it was the epic poet who had anticipated and hijacked his story instead of Rabindranath adapting the *Rāmāyaṇa* paradigm. He wrote: "I notice a similarity between the narrative direction of the *Rāmāyaṇa* and the plot outline of the present play. But the reason is not that the story has been gathered from the *Rāmāyaṇa*. The actual cause is that it is *Kaviguru* (the arché-poet) who has stolen my story *a priori* by means of his imaginative foresight. If you ask me what is the proof, I shall tell you, nobody will accept that during his time the golden citadel of Lanka was manifest with such enormous towering heights. That it is a phenomenon essentially of our times, remains evident as they lie scattered in thousands of proofs in thousands of instances." In this context one can just cite Harold Bloom's observation which should be self-explanatory: "But poetic influence need not make poets less original; as often it makes them more original..." (Bloom 7).

(iii) Points of comparison

Indeed there are some interesting points of comparison and contrast between Valmiki's epic and Tagore's play.

(a) The basic plot of the *Rāmāyaṇa* is constituted by the abduction of Sita, and the consequent destruction of Lanka. Tagore's play too seems to reify the epic plot within the compact space of the play—by the arrival of Nandini in the Yakshapuri and the consequent fall of the Yakshapuri.

(b) The similarity between the king of Lanka and the king of Yakshapuri has been underscored by the author himself.

(c) The *Rakshasas* in the epic are averse to agriculture and votaries for accumulation through plundering. The analogy can be legitimately extended to the principles of Yakshapuri which depends for its survival and prosperity upon digging and accumulation of wealth hidden inside the bowels of the earth.

(d) In both the epic and the play the basic conflict can also be envisioned as the conflict between man and machine. Rabindranath envisioned the Rakshasa civilization as a kind of machine-civilization.

These are of course ideas finely suggested by the play rather than explicitly stated. However, in his personal observations outside the text Tagore has repeatedly foregrounded the analogy and parallels.

Themes and Thematics

(i) Machine

Tagore wrote in *Rāśiār Cithi* (Letter from Russia):

> Since the time it became possible to multiply profit enormously with the help of machine, the medieval

> ideal of chivalry or the heroic ideal has been made to give way to the ideal of trade and commerce. The inception of the trading era is marked by plundering. The earth had shrieked at the horrid plundering of slaves and treasure that day. Since then the throne of Kuber has been entrenched in the world. Science announced that the rule of machine was the rule of the world; there was no other eternal truth beyond explicit profit-making. The arrogance of competition became pervasive, robbery acquired the prestige of a respectable vocation. Through visible and secret avenues, in the factories, mines, sprawling farms disguised slavery is being carried on, alongside falsehood and fierce cruelty. In the West those who amass money and those who supply it are now about to confront one another in a violent showdown.

Tagore had indeed felt increasingly concerned by the direction, or better to say 'misdirection' that civilization seemed to be taking in the modern times of industry, as the machine was set for pushing the man out. He writes:

> The pressure of ruthless competition makes the workers subordinate to machine. We get stupefied by seeing the huge arrangement of civilization from outside. The terrible genocide that is going on all the time underneath the structure remains hidden. But it cannot be hidden from God; and some news of the consequence can be heard every now and then through social upheavals....
>
> By magnifying the enterprise of work to any extent, by hugely inflating the works, by throwing them into hostile encounter, the poison of unrest and grievance seethes up. The way men have to live crammed up in a mass inside and around these monstrous factories, emitting black smoke, that they are divested of their natural right to space. One's minimum privacy is lost. There is no scope for the necessary space, or time, or contemplation. Thus man gets unaccustomed to his own company, and consequently at the least break from work they strain to get rid of themselves by indulging in

> drink and other distraction. All lose the capacity of slipping into silence, stillness, joy.... On the other hand the privileged ones are tired out by the ceaseless pursuit of fresh excitements...and fail to see self and the world clearly. Everything is seen hazily.
>
> (*Nababarṣa* [The New Year]. *Dharma*; my translation)

The discourse on drink by Fagulal and Bishu in the play can be read alongside this observation. Fagulal first appears on the stage looking for the bottle which his wife has hidden. This is a rare holiday, and he wants his bottle in the very morning hour. Bishu can understand this thirst through his own experience:

> *Bishu.* To that boundless tavern, underneath the blue canopy? Alas, the road is closed.... No open sky, no leisure for us; so we have distilled the essence of all the song and laughter, all the sunlight of the twelve hours' day into one draught of liquid fire. (13)

Anyway, it would be wrong perhaps to assume that the play pleads for total rejection of the machine; rather it seems to highlight the need of some sort of balance,—balance between machine and life, power and love, duty and joy in order to ensure fullness of life. But if, for some reason the machine overpowers a society, then that society is headed for destruction, unless this is stopped by the arrival of some Nandini, i.e. the principle of joy. Yaksha Town is such a society where the machine has become all powerful and thereby set to oppress and dehumanize man.

Again, it will certainly be reductive reading if the play is taken to be exclusively concerned about industrialism. Industrialism of course provides the immediate situation; but, looked deeper it seems to be about the conflict between insensitized heart and the call of life as well. Owing to the excess of domination by machine under industrialism man becomes insensitive to what is good and what is evil/detrimental for man, and thus becomes usable tools in the hands of the powerful. Industrialism serves to underscore this issue in the context of the play. But at bottom it is the clash between the principles of vibrant life and inert matter. Nandini represents this vibrancy of life, whereas the total life of the Yaksha Town has rejected this natural urge for natural life and thereby turned inert. Similar paradigm has been worked out again and again in Tagore's plays in which the action revolves around this basic conflict between life and death, flow and stagnation, vibrancy and inertness. The inordinate desire for power renders man insensitive to the good—this is what has been shown in *Free Water*. And the excess of machine orientation renders man lifeless, dull, mechanical; digging up handfuls of dead gold turns man into a dull lifeless mass—this is shown in *Red Oleanders*.

Tagore wrote in 1933:

> There is no meaning in such words as spiritualising the machine; we can spiritualise our own being which makes use of the machine.... Today the profit that the machine brings to our door is too big and we do not hesitate to scramble for it even at the cost of our humanity. The shrinking of the man in us is concealed by the augmentation of things outside and we lack the time to grieve over the loss.... The means that science has produced through which to gain access into Nature's storehouse is tremendously complex which... makes it not only unavailable to the majority of mankind but also compels us to centralise it in monster factories, uprooting the workers' life from its natural soil creating unhappiness....
>
> ...What is called progress is the progress in the mechanical contrivances; it is in fact an indefinite extension of our physical limbs and organs which, owing to the enormous material advantage that it brings to us has tempted the modern man away from his inner realm of spiritual value and thus the balance is lost....
>
> ('Can Science be Humanized?' *EWT* 7:904)

The runners of the system are of blunt shallow efficiency, "who presume to buy human souls with their money and throw them into their dustbins when they have been sucked dry..." ('Can Science be Humanized?' *EWT* 7:905). Precisely this same idea is hinted by the left-over of the king (*rājār ẽto*), the drained battered men churned out by the monstrous machine of Yakshapuri.

In a way, the play is about the impact of machine upon human mind. However, it is not so much about machine, as about the consequent social crisis generated by a machine-dependent civilization.

(ii) Science

Tagore had felt deep anxiety about man's handling of science, i.e. scientific knowledge and resources. He felt science has given man enormous power; with the help of science man today is metaphorically in possession of ten heads and thousand eyes like the legendary demon. But the problem is that man does not know how to mobilize and engage this power towards activities which should be beneficial for himself. He fails to strike a balance between the forces of life and those of machine. Hence the accumulating fatigue that was about to weigh down civilization. Although Tagore appreciated the West's scientific pursuit, he felt apprehensive as well; because he perceived:

> Their [the West] enterprise and boldness does not want to accept any limit to its own demand. One by one they have been discovering all the hidden mysteries of the world, measuring it, weighing it, and taking possession of it. It is by means of their own strength that they have broken into nature's great storehouse of energy, and greedily plundering that treasure....
>
> It is because the pride of Europe regarding its own power has swelled to an extreme that it has no time to consider where its dearth lies. In a land where external nature is excessively imposing or overpowering, human mind gets overwhelmed by it, and becomes self-oblivious; similarly man gets infatuated by the exorbitantly huge volume of his self-accumulated mass of matter and external façade, and thus starts his own defeat. In course of the continuous erosion of the harmony of the mind under the weight of the external

> mass a day comes when man's prosperity crumbles down in a terrible disaster to kiss the dust....
>
> Where science serves to alleviate the misery and need of the common people, science attains nobility. But where it is engaged specially to make some person or race rich or powerful, that is the mark of its terrible fall; because our conscience is clouded then, and putting on the armor of big names like patriotism, nationalism, etc, it launches fight against itself. Consequently all over the world today the relationship between the races is thrown off the balance... The state polity, while disseminating political pestilence, gets corrupted inside under the pollution of cruelty and deceit.
>
> (*Swādhikārapramatta. Kālāntar*; my translation)

That Tagore had this apprehension at the back of his mind, this unease and anxiety, while writing the play becomes evident from his own later comments with reference to the play:

> Science has permeated Western life; it no longer has its own cradle in the secluded cells of the learned. In a similar manner, the hungry purpose, having science for its steed, running about unchecked, trampling our life's harvest, is not an intellectual generalization unfit for imaginative literature. It is intensely real; its hot breath is upon us; its touch is all over our shrinking soul. It is the principal hero to-day in the drama of human history; and I trust I have the right to invoke it in my own play, not in the spirit of a politician, but of a poet, possibly a lyrical poet. (see Appendix ii)

(iii) Woman

Rabindranath writes in *Yātrī* with reference to the idea expressed in *Raktakarabi*: "In Yakshapur(sic) the enormous strength of man wrenches up the golden treasure from under the earth. The greedy enterprise of ruthless accumulation has driven out the sweetness of life from the place. By getting entwined in his own trap of complexity man has alienated himself from the world. So he has forgotten that joy is more precious than gold; he has forgotten that there is no fullness to be offered by power. Love alone can bring fulfillment. The huge arrangement there to keep man enslaved has also led to the self-imprisonment of the slave-runner. At such a turn the woman arrives there; Nandini arrives. The force of life confronted the machine. The surge of love began to assault the imprisoning net of avaricious misadventure. Then, how at the mysterious inspiration of the woman did the man set to overthrow the prison of his own making and thereby release the flow of life—this is described in the play". (my translation)

Rabindranath had a conviction about the mutual complementarity of the male and female principles. Such perfect balance is indeed rare in reality. In Yakshapuri the male energy swells to enormity as he sets for the target of invincibility through irrefutable machine. So, to stop this suicidal venture the woman arrives there, Nandini arrives as the symbol of energy, life, love and joy.

In drawing points of comparison between his own play and Valmiki's epic Tagore highlights the role of a mortal woman in the ultimate defeat of the demonic power. 'Ravana', the great accumulator and possessor in the *Tretāyug*, had kept in chain even the deities with lightning and thunder, and made them work for him. His rule could go on unchallenged for ever. But suddenly a mortal girl appeared amidst his god-defying prosperity and at once justice was stirred. He[Rama] defeated the Rakshasha with ignorant, unarmed monkeys. Not exactly the same has taken place in my play; but here too a mortal girl makes her appearance (trans. Present writer). Tagore makes an unambiguous assertion of his conviction in this regard as he writes with reference to the play: "When the woman's lively energy, in its multiple sweet dimensions, is obstructed against instilling the male ventures, then the machine takes over. Then man only hurts and gets hurt by the blow of the machine of his own creation."

Rabindranath argued: "In the woman of the Western world a certain restlessness is noticed which cannot be the normal aspect of her nature. For women who want something special and violent in their surroundings to keep their interests active only prove that they have lost touch with their own true world" ('Personality: Woman', *EWT:* 7). Tagore expressed his conviction:

> She must restore the lost social balance by putting the full weight of the woman into the creation of the human world...woman must come to the bruised and maimed world of the individual ('Personality: Woman')
>
> Woman can bring her fresh mind and all her power of sympathy to this new task of building up a spiritual civilization, if she will be conscious of her responsibilities. ('Personality: Woman')

Tagore further claimed in this connection that "the masculine creations of intellectual civilization are towers of Babel, they dare to defy their foundations and therefore topple down over and over again" ('Personality: Woman'); and "woman's function is the passive function of the soil, which not only helps the tree grow but keeps its growth within limits". ('Personality: Woman')

However, one cannot overlook the fact that in the play it is only Nandini who stands up to this model, whereas Chandra represents another aspect of the female principle; it is the negative, limited, possessive person. Tagore also throws hint about the former wife of Bishu who had allured him to make for this cursed city. There are the wives of the governors, who apparently enjoy the cream of the system. The author makes no attempt to cover up the greed for gold among these women, which may have further contributed to the pervasive 'gold rush' of their male partners.

> *Chandra.* ...you men have gone to the dogs in Yaksha Town...but we women haven't changed at all.
>
> *Bishu.* Haven't you? Your flowers have faded, and you are all slavering for gold.
>
> *Chandra.* No, never!
>
> *Bishu.* I say, yes. That Phagulal toils over and above the twelve,—why? For a reason unknown to him, unknown even to you. But I know. It's your dream of gold that lashes him on to work, more severely than the foreman's whip. (13-14)

Bishu knows even the will to flee the place has been destroyed; so he tells Chandra:

> If you go there (home) today you will fly back here tomorrow, like a caged bird to its cage, hankering for its drugged food. (14)

Except Nandini no other woman, neither Chandra nor the governors' wives, registers any protest against the system.

(iv) Search

Everybody in Yakshapuri seems to be engaged in some search. The professor is looking for the meaning of dead words in his dry manuscripts; the diggers are desperately looking around amidst the dark bowel of the earth for gold; Nandini has been searching for Ranjan; the king himself, behind the net, is engaged in a self-searching without himself being aware of it.

(v) The polarization

In the polarization presented in both the epic and the play, there is the sweetness of life on one side, whereas on the other there is self-destructive wealth; on one side there is joy, as implied by the names,—'Rama' and 'Ranjan'; Rama is one who gives joy, Ranjan is one who brings color to the mind; on the other side there are Ravana, and the supremo of Yakshapuri.

Again, Rama has made Sita his own through love; Ravana's avaricious possessiveness has led to her abduction. And like Ravana, intent on snapping the deep bond of love between Sita and Rama, the ruler of the machine realm in *Red Oleanders* also is bent upon tearing the lovers apart in his greedy, confused jealousy/envy.

Chandra, Phagulal, Bishu are also unhappy dissenters, but their dissent does not have the firmness; it is not prompted by the clarity of vision that we find in Nandini, or the strength of Ranjan that we hear about. The other oppositional tenor has been provided by the harvesting song floating in from the distant fields.

(vi) Message of hope

In the clash between individual vs. organized power, none emerges winner or defeated at the end. Coming out from behind his net, the first thing the King does is breaking the flagstaff, and then joining the rebel diggers against his own establishment run by the administrative executives: the Governor, Headman, Gosai. When Phagulal seeks to clarify, "we are out to break your own prison", the King says: "Yes, it is my *own* prison. You and I must work together, for you cannot break it alone".

Phagulal. As soon as the Governor hears of it, he will march with all his forces to prevent us.

King. Yes, my fight is against them.

Phagulal. But the soldiers will not obey you.

King. You will be on my side!

Phagulal. Shall we be able to win through?

King. We shall at least be able to die! At last I have found the meaning of death. I am saved! (50)

Tagore wrote elsewhere:

> We must know with absolute certainty that essentially we are spiritual. This we can do by winning mastery over self, by rising above all pride and greed and fear, by knowing that worldly losses and physical death can take nothing away from the truth and greatness of our soul. The chic knows when it breaks through the self-centred isolation of its egg that the hard shell which covered it so long was not really a part of its life. That shell is a dead thing, it has no growth; it affords no glimpse whatever of the vast beyond that lies outside it. However pleasantly perfect and rounded it may be, it must be given a blow to, it must be burst through and thereby the freedom of light and air be won, and the complete purpose of bird life be achieved. (*Sādhanā*)

Shambhu Mitra writes: "Rabindranath had envisioned the humiliation of the individual in the face of organized power. He had hoped man's irrepressible force of life would ultimately save him. Perhaps. But even then he had mentioned the waste of so much harvest as it falls scattered on the dust" (my translation). Mitra draws attention to Tagore's awareness of the waste that is involved in the process.

Ultimately the King succeeds in breaking through his iron net. Freedom is achieved from the gigantic system of machine-ruled materiality. Though this freedom comes at tremendous cost—the death of Ranjan and Kishore—vibrant youth and innocent boyhood, still it signals the message—howsoever confused/overpowered man may get under the rule of machine and materialism, his basic life-force is never destroyed altogether. Sooner or later it will resurface at the inspiration of life; Nandini ushers in that inspiration of life.

One should not, however, miss the fact that Tagore had taken care to point out repeatedly that the book was a vision and not a propaganda.

> I can assure my readers that I never meant to use this book as propaganda. It is a vision that has come to me in the darkest hour of dismay. I have a stronger faith in the simple personality of man than in the prolific brood of machinery that wants to crowd it.

Furthermore, he maintains,

> This personality—the divine essence of the infinite in the vessel of the finite—has its last treasure-house in woman's heart. Her pervading influence will some day restore the human to the desolated world of man. As in the animal world the physically meek has to-day inherited the earth, woman will one day prove that the meek in soul, through the sure power of love, will rescue this world from the dominance of the unholy spirit of rapacity. The joy of this faith has inspired me to pour all my heart into painting against the background of black shadows—the nightmare of a devil's temptation—the portrait of Nandini as the bearer of the message of reality, the saviour through death. (Appendix ii)

Some critics have conjectured about the possibility of the impact on Tagore's imagination of Delacroix's famous painting (1830) of the fall of Bastille during the French Revolution (1789), in which the rebellious crowd is shown as being led by a peasant woman.

Characters

Anonymity, Names, Naming

Roland Barthes in his S/Z mentions the anonymity of the Proustian narrator, "his perilously maintained lack of name", which he thinks, "creates a serious deflation of the realistic illusion" (Barthes 102). Here anonymity largely prevails among the citizens barring just a few proper names. They are not, as it were, fully alive, but only shadowy presences swaying about in the 'death's dream kingdom' of this nightmarish domain. In his talk to Elmherst in 1924 Tagore observed: "This is a world where, with every available means in his power, the Great King exploits the resources of the underworld, of nature, of the mind, of science and of human physique and intelligence, using all the weapons of organization and the elaborate machinery of a highly centralized bureaucracy in order to add to his wealth. This wealth he measures in gold, or in souls or in facts, or in human bodies, so that *men are men no longer but numbers.*" (emphasis added)

The diggers say, once they were persons when they were in their home-village; now they have become numbers. 'We are not men to them, but numbers' (15). Phagulal is No. 47 V, Bishu is 69 Ng. The Governor addresses Bishu as 'Hullo, 69 Ng' (16). Governor and Gosain exchange notes about different slums and people in terms of their respective numbers:

> *Governor.* Parish T-D. No. 71 T is headman there. It ends to the left of where No. 65 of Row M lives.
>
> *Gosain.* My son, though Parish T-D may not yet be quieted, the whole row of M's have lately become steeped in…meekness. (18)

Gosain also addresses Phagulal as 'friend 47 V'. This is obviously much more than funny number game; it points to a grim reality of the situation. The bulk of personae here are not individualized; they represent one or another group/category in the hierarchy of the place. This shows how under the impact of machine human distinctiveness and uniqueness are on the wane. In this society, built up on the basis of avarice, "which is not social in character, but utilitarian" (Tagore), everything seems to have been set in order to fit into some prescribed pattern. This applies not only to the area plan, but also to the humans. The moment they enter the factory, i.e. the system, they get reduced to abstract numbers. The other, prior identities fall redundant. The localities are known and mentioned in terms of abstraction: T-D parish or M parish, and the residents are known as numbers (Huxley: *Brave New World*; Orwell; the politics of naming). With the advent of industrialization the workers were displaced from their village and forced to live by the factory. In the village they were free workers in control of their own schedule. Here they are forced to follow the schedule of the factory; furthermore while in the village the whole family could work together, now they are separated, fragmentized. Hence the nostalgia of the workers for the 'home', when they cannot go home any more.

Those who are not numbers, are mentioned by their vocation instead of a personal name: Professor, Gosain, Physician, etc. It is the epitome of regimented life. Even the 'King' seems to have been cast in the same paradigmatic design of anonymity. In this connection one can recall Tagore's anxiety over the elimination of the 'personal' from institutions.

> To-day another factor has made itself immensely evident in shaping and guiding human destiny. It is the spirit of organization, which is not social in character, but utilitarian. Christian Europe no longer depends upon Christ for her peace, but upon the league of Nations, because her peace is not disturbed by forceful individuals so much as by organised Powers. Naturally, in all organizations, variation of personality is eliminated, and the individual members, in so far as they represent the combination to which they belong, give expression to a common type and very little to their uniqueness of individuality.

Tagore's critique of this regimentation is reflected in a significant aspect of the play which had drawn the attention of Shambhu Mitra's playing troupe: each of those whom the authority does not consider human, and sees only as numbers, has been conferred individual names by the playwright; for instance, Phagulal, Chandra, Bishu, Gokul, *et al.* Thus Bishu, who is just 69 Ng to the establishment gets back his own name among friends, along with the distinction of an additional epithet—'pagal'. On the other hand, the bosses, who do not take cognizance of these commoners as individuals, have been given only the brand-name of their vocation; for instance, Governor, Deputy Governor, Professor, Physician, Moṛol (Headman), etc. Only Gosain is given a first name; and that name is 'Kenaram'; Mitra wonders if the name 'Kenaram' which means 'a purchasable person', a man with a price tag, is a name or an epithet, because 'he takes the name of God, but takes the food from the Governor' (*RO*).

In contrast to the average residents of the place Nandini is individual. So are Ranjan and Kishor. Significantly, the most important person remains a 'Voice' and 'King', without a personal name. The 'personal man' is apparently forced to take the backseat by the 'organised man' in him.

Individuals

Nandini

Nandini is one of those characters who are simultaneously individuals and symbols.

Nandini occupies the centre-stage through the play; in a way it might be considered the story of a woman called 'Nandini'. She gets revealed against the backdrop of pervasive oppression all around. She is like the fountain which bursts up beautifully through the very obstacles, and sends its sprays of laughter, tear, melody all around and high upwards. The very life it registers by the burst is enthralling and liberating with its beauty, splendour, daring. Nandini is the liberating force in Yakshapuri. Nandini arrives in this dead place as the symbol of energy, life, love and joy. Where does she hail from? The author has left it vague.

The semantic meaning of the name is a girl/daughter/giver of joy; because daughter gives joy; this is further related to aesthetics, the principle of beauty; the beauty which has its appeal to all through joy.

Again, Nandini's close connection with the earth has been carefully highlighted. Nandini's costume, the fresh flowers on her hair and neck, her rural way of donning a sari, which is again of the color of ripe paddy; this is also another variation of the color of gold—not flashy or dazzling, but soothing, subdued; the background music of harvesting greeting her ears and making her restive.

Rama and Ravana in the epic come to clash on account of the abduction of Sita. In the play the same event resurfaces as an idea. Here the clash takes place between the votaries of growing plant and the band for plundering underground wealth. Tagore points out, Sita suggests the line of the furrow opening before the plough; and thereby Sita manifests the agricultural ways. The two communities with two opposite cultures clash upon this 'Sita'. Tagore's own play too veers round in course of the action upon the clash between two opposite ways of life; and it is Nandini who sets it snowballing.

The poet has left hints in the play that Nandini does not belong to the dark world underground where people search for hidden treasure. She belongs to the zone of light, upon the earth's surface, where beauty dances, love ripples at ease; Nandini is part of that simple easeful happiness and beauty.

Nandini represents a dynamic life-energy-emotion; and thus lends dynamism to the action. It is because of her that ripples are sent through the stagnant situation. So long things were following the same dull, monotonous, repetitive course; but as Nandini enters the scene people begin to react in various ways. Nandini is an anachronism in the place; so some would try to appropriate her, whereas others would prefer to drive her out of the domain. The play starts at this point. Tagore writes: "sometimes by accident some uneatable aquatic creatures happen to get caught in the fishermen's net; not only do they refuse to fill the stomach or the pocket; in course they tear off the net itself. A girl named Nandini has chanced to step into the web of incidents in this play. The façade shielding Makarraj is about to collapse with her advent" (trans. present writer).

Nandini can connect with different kinds of people with perfect ease, naturally, without inhibition, yet she is never without an innate dignity, although at one point she gets so infuriated that she would tear off Gosain's rosary and wrap, and admonish Governor in unambiguous terms: "Aren't you afraid of me, because I am a woman? God sends His thunderbolt through His messenger, the lightning spark—that bolt I have borne here with me; it will shatter the golden spire of your mastery" (37).

But Tagore would rather not present her as an abstraction: "I am glad to find that my critics readily acknowledge that Nandini, the heroine of the play, has definite features of an individual person. She is not an abstraction, but is pursued by an abstraction, like one tormented by a ghost. And this is the drama. Nandini is a real woman who knows that wealth and power are *māyā*, and that the highest expression of life is in love, which she manifests in her love for Ranjan" (Tagore: Appendix ii).

The other characters can be understood in terms of their respective responses to the event of Nandini's arrival in Yakshapuri; because they have been presented precisely that way.

The King

A 'King' often makes his presence in Tagore's plays. But the King of *Red Oleanders* is unique in his own way, and cannot be reconciled with the images of the 'King' in *Post Office*, or the King in *King of the Dark Chamber* or *Phālgunī*. Tagore himself had said, "Thanks to scientific power the limbs and heads of man have invisibly multiplied. There are hints in the play that the King of my Pala grabs and devours through this excess of power. So he had compared this King to the mythical demon king Ravana. Nandalal Basu, the renowned painter and an Ashramite during Tagore's time, defined the King as 'the scientific intelligence of today's man' (cited in Mitra). Tagore himself, in an interpretation of the play, mentions the King as an 'apparition' or 'abstraction' representing "megalomaniac ambition, while an acquisitive intellect plies its psychological curiosity, probing into the elusive mystery of love through vivisection" (Appendix ii).

The King is the supreme ruler of Yaksha Town which has been built by his strength alone. Though it is run by the governors, they do it for him; the diggers dig for him. People are sucked out until reduced to skin and bones because he would rise big. He stays behind a net, beyond the access of all. Several questions can stir in the reader/spectator's mind while following the play:

(1) Is it of his own accord that he keeps behind the net? Or, is it according to the plan of the governors, who may have found this system advantageous to their interest?

(2) It is the governors who appear the keenest to defend status quo for the system; then is it possible that they enjoy the cream out of the King's enterprises?

(3) Is the change at the end inconsistent with the earlier impression we get about the King? In connection with this issue it may be pointed out that the King is not mean; he is not selfish or heartless. That is why he is the King; he has the regality, the towering dignity, the peerless strength. As the play starts already chinks are showing up, fissures have appeared in the solid structure of his strength. In course of the play he arrives at self-knowledge; but the process has started with the very start of the play; therefore, it seems only natural that when the chance comes he should lose no time in prevarication; he can instantly declare war against the very system he has built up himself day by day.

(4) Shambhu Mitra, whose production of *Raktakarabī* had been a memorable event for the Bengali stage, interprets the King, following Nandalal Basu, as the symbol of science. One wonders, however, if this is an adequate explanation/definition of the person who seems more an enigma than a real human.

(5) Is it possible to relate the symbolic king to the author himself at the time, just as Nandini can be traced back to the lively beautiful little girl Ranu, and Ranjan to the delightful lively young Elmherst? [Incidentally, the play was dedicated to Elmherst.] Nirod C. Chaudhuri hints at the poet being weighed down by the pressure of work, a lonely alien inside, helpless prisoner of his own public image, fatigued

> at meeting demands from all quarters, yet aware of the impossibility of cutting through the prison-bar, metaphorically speaking (*Ātmaghātī Rabīndranāth*); the existentialist angst of the song of Tagore, *Āmi jato bhār jamiye tulechi sakali hayeche bojhā*, and the appeal, *e bojhā āmār nāmāo bandhu nāmāo* can also be recalled in the context. ["Whatever I have amassed has become such a wearisome burden! Oh my friend, help me to put down the burden!"] (my translation)

The King is ambivalent in his response to Nandini; he is simultaneously attracted and repelled by her, drawn towards her and repulsed away. Nandini fascinates him; yet he would also be relieved if he could drive her away. Where the King is the ruler of Yakshapuri, where he is the biggest machine of all the machines in the place, Nandini repels him. The King has a hunch this girl has come to put a stop to his machine-oriented activity.

However, there is also a hidden self within the hidden King; from behind his impenetrable net, the man in the King, his human heart, occasionally stirs and becomes eager for the touch of another human heart; it is in this self that he feels the tremendous pull of Nandini. He is constituted by the opposites of the machine and human, and is torn between the opposite pulls.

The King appears to command limitless strength. This has been further reinforced by intelligence and scientific resources, thereby enhancing his strength to any degree. Yet he is torn by opposite pulls of the right inspiration and wrong motives. Amidst his vast material prosperity a girl steps in. She proves instrumental in stirring up the potential Bibhisan within the Ravana, the dormant human instinct within the acquired scientific power. Finally, the former triumphs over the latter.

The King is weighed down by the fatigue that accumulates through the failure to reconcile science with life. This is the cause of his attraction towards Nandini, and the consequent jealousy against Ranjan. It is the longing of one who is exhausted by machine for the pure free life.

How the machine, by absorbing all the energy, leads to stagnation instead of dynamism can be seen in the predicament of the king. Though ceaseless activity is going on in the place, the King, who is supposed to be the centre of all these activities, is himself fixed/static behind the net of his own making. Thus the machine, which was manufactured to enhance man's activity, eventually robs him of the dynamic energy, and imprisons him. It is only after breaking through the net that he recovers his own initiative.

Tagore writes: "In my Pala (a folkform of play in India) there is a king. In this modern age I could not dare to give him more than one head and two arms. I would if I had the kind of confidence enjoyed by the prime poet; indeed thanks to the power of science the count of man's limbs and head has invisibly multiplied. There are hints in the play to suggest that the king of my Pala grabs and possesses by means of that very excess of strength" (my translation).

Tagore's King, however, is more complex than Ravana in the sense that he includes within himself the traits of Bibhishana too, the brother of Ravana in the epic who had rejected Ravana's ways and deserted his camp. It is a subtler and profounder concept that the King manifests in the play. If the King is a modern version of Ravana, then the Bibhishana, his other self, resides not outside, but within him; it had been dormant so long, and now wakes up at the call of Nandini, her repeated knockings on his iron net. Ultimately a time comes when he tears the net apart and comes out to declare rebellion against the lifeless crushing system created by himself.

Tagore writes: "There was no dearth of space in the seven Books of the First poet; therefore he had allotted separate places/roles to Ravana and Bibhishana. But he had also left the hint that they were the same, they were siblings. Inside the same nest sin and its lethal destructor have been nurtured. In my slim play the present incarnation of Ravana is both Ravana and Bibhishana in the same person. He defeats but himself…".

This King, like two other kings of Tagore's two other plays, *Arūpratan* and *Dākghar*, remains invisible though his voice is audible. He hides himself in the darkness or behind the curtain of iron net. Like the other two, this king also becomes visible at the end. But unlike the other two he has been terrifying; and when he finally emerges,—breaking the door open, tearing the net apart—he has rebelled against the system of his own making. This process of self-concealment eventually ending in self-revelation has been identified by Ashrukumar Sikdar as a common motif in Rabindranath's play.

However, the King continues to be apprehensive of his other self since the beginning of the play; he is afraid to come outside; he cannot relate himself to the earth, the corn, the golden light. Nandini calls out to him: "You too come out, King!—out into the fields." The 'Voice' floats out: "Fields! What could I do there?" He has lost the skill of doing simple things, as he moans, "It is the simple which is impossible for me. A lake cannot run out dancing, like a frolicsome waterfall..." (8).

Yet he commands amazing strength which fascinates Nandini; as she explains: "The day you let me into your store-house the blocks of gold did not surprise me,—what amazed me was the immense strength with which you lifted and arranged them" (8).

There is, again, a subtle connection between the King and Ranjan. Ranjan is youth incarnate. The King too had once built up the huge system with the strength of his youth, which attracts Nandini. But she wants that enormous strength of the King to be engaged to create new living civilization instead of piling up dead wealth and erecting a dead system.

In the final analysis the King emerges as a human individual; once he had youth but now it is gone. His pain, his anger, his confusion all together make him a living individual in spite of his endless mystery. The King's progress in the play can be understood in the light of Tagore's observation in another context: "Man grows gigantic by the appropriation of everything for himself: he attains harmony by giving himself up" (*EWT* 5:20).

King and Nandini

This attainment, however, would not have been possible without the intervention of Nandini. When Nandini speaks of the 'curse' involved in rending the earth's bosom, the king seems not to understand; he seems to be rather proud and even boastful of his strength. "But we bring up strength. Does not my strength please you Nandini?" (8). The King has acquired this strength; yet he does not seem satisfied. He is annoyed by 'the mystery' of Nandini's beauty which he fails to grasp. This is the limitation of science; it can measure, weigh, analyze but cannot feel. "I want to pluck you out of it (evasion), to grasp you within my closed fist, to handle you, scrutinize you,—or else to break you to pieces." Hence his restiveness, his anger: "Why can't I strain out the tint of your oleanders and build a dream out of it to keep before my eyes? Those few frail petals guard it and hinder me. Within you there is the same hindrance, so strong because so soft…" (8).

This can be read alongside Tagore's observation: "The view that we can get of her (the West), in our mutual dealings, is that of a titanic power with an endless curiosity to analyse and know; but without sympathy to understand; with numberless arms to coerce and acquire, but no serenity of soul to realise and enjoy" (Appendix i).

Apparently, prior to meeting Nandini, the King had not been aware of his extreme fatigue, which seems to have suddenly flashed upon him with overpowering effect, and stirs Nandini's awe and sympathy.

> I, who am a desert, stretch out my hand to you, a tiny blade of grass, and cry: I am parched, I am bare, I am weary. The flaming thirst of this desert licks up one fertile field after another, only to enlarge itself,—it can never annex the life of the frailest of grasses. (9-10)

He again adds, as if in a self-absorbed slow interior monologue, looking into a mirror:

> One day, Nandini, in a far off land, I saw a mountain as weary as myself. I could not guess that all its stones were aching inwardly. One night I heard a noise, as if some giant's evil dream had moaned and moaned and suddenly snapped asunder. Next morning I found the mountain had disappeared in the chasm of a yawning earthquake. That made me understand how overgrown power crushes itself inwardly by its own weight. (10)

It is through this fatigue that he perceives in Nandini what he lacks himself, in spite of all his wealth,—"the dance rhythm of the All" (10). The 'Voice' of the invisible King here gets conflated by the voice of the poet of *Gitanjali*, as he defines the 'rhythm':

> The rhythm that lightens the enormous weight of matter. To that rhythm the bands of stars and planets go about dancing from sky to sky, like so many minstrel boys. It is that rhythm, Nandini, that makes you so simple, so perfect. How small you are compared to me, yet I envy you. (10)

In course of, his enterprise "to plunder the world's big treasure-houses", he has been self-alienated from this 'rhythm of all', and would still greedily long for the mystery of the rhythm. He can guess there are gifts that Nandini's "little flower-like fingers can easily reach, but not all the strength" of his body,—"gifts hidden in God's closed hand". He still hopes to possess it by means of force,—"That hand I must force open some day". He would implore Nandini for just a touch of her little hand, and then again lapse back to his drudgery, his schedule of "busy time, overloaded with work, dragged along against obstruction." He seems to know somehow this 'time' is not fit for receiving Nandini. The above dialog between the 'Voice' and Nandini, which discloses the erosion that has already undermined the King's stability, also carries hints of a forthcoming crisis in which the strong façade of the King's nature will collapse. It becomes clear at this stage that the King suffers from a sense of frustration, which makes him fly into sudden spurts of anger, and again relapse into sadness, almost into bleak despair of a beggar, and again getting bitter and demonic in his envy of Ranjan.

King and Ranjan: Contrast and Connection

During his talk with Nandini across the network, the King says rather resentfully, "In me there is only strength, in Ranjan there is magic." As the play starts, a conflict has already set in the king; he boasts of his power, yet it seems he does not enjoy thus amassing strength. Already he has a glimpse of the futility of his acquirements: "All I possess is so much dead weight"

(9). He feels tired (which he expresses in images of a desert, a sinking mountain). He does not want to force Nandini into subjection, yet he would occasionally lapse into the show of strength. Perhaps once he had youth, but now that youth is missing; instead what remains is strength, only strength. So he envies Ranjan. Even after Nandini admits his strength "makes my heart dance within me", the King must know if it is the same feeling that Ranjan stirs in her. As Nandini says, "that dance rhythm is different, you won't understand", the King would insist like some willful child, 'I will, I must understand' (9). He must know if Nandini likes him 'the same as Ranjan'.

The King is envious of Ranjan's youth, but fails to understand the secret of his youth, his magic, which resides in his connection with the rhythm of the universe. He has already identified his own lack, but that makes him only more resentful and fretful. "No increase of power can ever come up to youth. I can only guard by force"; it is at this point that he keenly feels inferior to Ranjan: "If I had Rañjan's youth I could leave you free and yet hold you fast. My time is spent in knotting the binding rope, but, alas, everything else can be kept tied, except joy" (9).

Ranjan

Ranjan and the King are connected by some mysterious thread of affinity. Nandini loves Ranjan, and yet feels a strange attraction for the King as well, though this is not exactly love. Ranjan is the essence of youth, held high above material and machine. On the other hand, the King is one whose essence has been caught and controlled by the machine; hence he has become unreal, which is epitomized by his invisibility behind iron net. Nandini, who manifests the exuberance of life, can love only Ranjan, the essential free man; she can have amazement, even a mild infatuation for the King; but her pure, eager, flowing love is reserved for Ranjan alone. So when the King reaches out for her flowers she refuses, because "Some one loves red oleanders and calls me by that name". She makes it clear—"It is in remembrance of him that I wear these flowers" (26), an answer that annoys and angers the King. At the end, it is to Ranjan that she sends her bangle of Raktakarabi.

In answer to the King's query—how does she love Ranjan, Nandini says, "I love Ranjan as the rudder in the water might love the sail in the sky, answering its rhythm of wind in the rhythm of waves" (23). If Nandini is beauty Ranjan is joy. Etymologically, the name suggests color and joy. Therefore he is irresistible like the wild stream. He can restore life into the realm of death. He is the laughter of God. His joy gets manifest in the exuberant energy of life. As Nandini describes—which is also a way of defining the mystery of his charm—

> ...he [Ranjan] holds an oar in each hand and ferries me across the stormy waters; he catches wild horses by the mane and rides with me through the woods; he shoots an arrow between the eyebrows of the tiger on the spring, and scatters my fear with loud laughter. As he jumps into our Nagai river and disturbs its current with his joyous splashing, so he disturbs me with his tumultuous life. Desperately he stakes his all on the game and thus has he won me. (21)

Whereas Nandini is the eternal primordial strength of life which finds expression through woman, Ranjan, symbolizes youth, which gives dynamism, motivation, inspiration to all human activity.

The Rulers and the Ruled

A common theme of Tagore's plays is that discipline is necessary; but when it becomes more hindrance than help in the blossoming of life then a crisis becomes imminent. Then the structure needs to be pulled down. But nothing else than the surge of life itself is adequate for the job. The same paradigm holds in *Muktadhārā* and *Acalāyatan*. In *Muktadhārā*, Prince Abhijit sacrifices his own life to release the waterfall from the bondage of machine.

Most of the minor personae in *Red Oleanders* are either completely under the rule of discipline, or they subscribe to the ideology of this autocracy and actively work for it; indeed they are the establishment of this domain.

Governor

Firstly, we can consider the Governors; again, even amongst the Governors, who enjoy a position of power in the total hierarchy of the autocratic system, there is yet another hierarchy, wheels within wheels, by which they are fixated in their specific positions—as the Governor, the Deputy Governor, and the Assistant Governor. These Governors are supposed to be efficient and competent persons. It is thanks to their alert administration that the Yaksha Town smoothly rolls along to unbroken prosperity. They run the place through the King. They serve to uphold and maintain the system. It is because of their ruthless service that the autocracy rules over the Yakshapuri. The system has dehumanized them and they in turn work hard to maintain and further strengthen the system. Thus they make a vicious coterie. They enjoy such tremendous power that once they get hold of something or someone even the King cannot loosen their bite.

Chandra. Why, he[Governor] seems to be so nice and—

Bishu. Yes, nice and polished, like the crocodile's teeth, which fit into one another with so thorough a bite that the King himself cannot unlock the jaw, even if he wants to. (16)

The Governors have used science and have become more powerful than science itself. They are extremely mischievous as one never knows how they would start mischief against whom, and under what pretext. Bishu says, "This place is dark with the Governor's shadow, it is everywhere" (23). [One can immediately recall the famous catch-phrase of Orwell's *1984*—'Big brother is watching you'.] Nandini says about the Governor, "I have never seen anything so lifeless,—like a cane stick cut from the cane bush,—no leaves, no roots, no sap in the veins" (23). Bishu follows with his rejoinder: "Cut off from life, he spends himself in repressing life" (23).

He is furthermore a dirty manipulator who can use any trick to trap and finish anyone. The thrashed wrestler is furious about the Governor, whose 'lying tongue' he would like to tear off. He knows what a mean schemer the Governor is,—set to destroy even the remnant of strength in a human. "They only feel safe when they rob the whole world of strength" (35). Therefore, although the wrestler had never wanted to fight, this Governor had egged him on, and now he says it is the former's fault. He mutters in impotent anger: 'If only once...I could fasten my teeth for once in the Governor's throat" (35). But actually he has no power to avenge himself over this man.

The Governor has no inhibition against selling absolute lies as truth. He sends message to Ranjan that the King has reduced Nandini to the status of royal concubine. Previously he had provoked Gajju the wrestler to challenge the King by means of some such falsehood. The Governor even cheats the King, as the King discovers at the end: "Deceived! These traitors have deceived me,—perdition take them! My own machine refuses my sway! Call the Governor—bring him to me handcuffed—" (47). But the Governor has his hand on the machine button; so even before the King can set out along with the rushing crowd of diggers set to break the prison, the Governor's troop can be heard approaching. The crashing noise can be heard above the charged atmosphere of the last scene.

Phagulal. King, do you hear the tumult?

King. There comes the Governor with his troops. How could he be so quick about it? He must have been prepared beforehand. They have used my power against me. (50)

Governor has absolutely no sense of guilt; he can glibly justify his wrongdoing by scientific analogies, and thus shirk off his responsibility in a crime he commits. To Nandini's anxious query, where has he taken Bishu, Governor replies callously:

> Who am I that I should take him? The wind carries off the clouds,—if you think that to be a crime, make enquiries as to who is behind the wind. (37)

Gosain

Chandra is taken in by the façade of Governor, the deceitful man,—'How he smiles every time he talks!' (18). But there is another around, who can beat even Governor in suave deceit; he is Gosain. Tagore wrote in *Nāṭyaparicay*: "Besides, there is one Gosainji. He takes the name of God, but he takes the food from the Governor. He contributes a lot to the well-being of the Yaksha Town" (trans. Present author). Gosain is also another Governor in disguise; he is part of this vicious establishment and perhaps the most obnoxious of the set of rulers, because of his cultivated hypocrisy. Deputy Governor tries to define the evasive Gosain:

> The poor man is really two in one, clumsily joined,—Priest on the skin, Governor at the marrow. He has to take precious care to prevent the Governor part of him coming up to the surface, lest it should clash too much with his telling of the beads. (43)

He is the religious man supposed to impart spiritual lessons to the diggers here. But his religious teachings are shaped so as to serve the interest of the autocratic establishment. It seems the two,—Governor and Gosain—are shrewdly acting rehearsed parts; the Governor informs the diggers, "I have sent for our High Preacher, Kenaram Gosain…to give moral talks to the men…", and at once Gosain enters the stage, as if he had been just waiting by the wings for the hint to drop in; Governor instantly starts ovation to a man who is but his employee, and can be 'sent for'. An obvious element of artificiality hangs low over their rehearsed conversation, carrying hints of a grim covert meaning under cover of the absurd pep-talk. One is reminded of the 'double-speak' of the *1984* Newspeak language nuances.

> *Governor.* Your Holiness, I do you reverence. These workmen of ours sometimes feel disturbed in their weak minds. Deign to whisper in their ears some texts of peace. The need is urgent.
>
> *Gosain.* These people? Are they not the very incarnation of the sacred Tortoise of our scripture, that held up the sinking earth on its back? Because they meekly suppress themselves underneath their burden, the upper world can keep its head afloat. The very thought sends a thrill through my body!

The hypocrite rolls on glibly:

> Just think of it, friend 47 V, yours is the duty of supplying food to this mouth which chants the holy

> name. With the sweat of your brow have you woven this wrap printed with the holy name, which exalts this devoted body. Surely that is no mean privilege. May you remain for ever undisturbed, is my benediction....
>
> My friends, repeat aloud the holy name of Hari, and all your burdens will be lighted.... (17)

Gosain is cynical in prostituting his 'religion' and oratory to the service of the oppressive establishment. Religion is not his goal; it is used as a clever ploy, an ideological devise, to justify the oppression. Like the sardars, he is just another guard of the system, only meaner and cleverer than others, showing the unholy alliance between 'Caesar and Church'. He is the parasite too: "Their votive fees will pay for his upkeep".

The man is characterized by an abominable innate vulgarity. Even as the wrestler lies broken in front of all he goes on talking about Nandini's garland of 'kund' flowers, as if the wounded man didn't exist. He mentions the garland with an overt vulgar thrust: "Ah indeed! The gift of a pure heart! God's own white kunda flowers! Their beauty remains unsullied even in the hands of a man of the world..." (36). To Nandini's urgent appeal to do something for the poor wrestler, Gosain says, "The Governor is sure to keep him as much alive as it is necessary for him to be. But, my child, these discussions will become your lips" (36). One feels disgusted, what gives him the right to speak in this tone to Nandini? Nandini is revolted at the suggestion of 'calculated apportioning of life'; but Gosain has no qualms to justify the evil system in God's own name: "Our class of people have their great burden to bear, therefore we have to claim a larger portion of life's sustenance for our share. That's according to Almighty God's own decree" (36). This anticipates the curious logic of the 'pigs' in Orwell's *Animal Farm* (1945) to justify their parasitic and exclusive consumption of the milk and apples, instead of sharing it with all the other animals,—and all this in the name of the 'cause': "We pigs are brain-workers. The whole management and organization of this farm depend on us. Day and night we are watching your welfare. It is for *your* sake that we drink that milk and eat those apples" (Orwell 22).

Assistant Governor

As he enters the stage for the first time, Governor calls out to him, rather brusquely, "Where are you going?" It seems Governor keeps his officers too under tight control, and they are answerable to him in this regimented hierarchical society. He proudly says, 'to arrest Ranjan', (an assignment initially given to Deputy Governor), as if this should be counted enough cause for bravado. Assistant Governor seems to be a familiar type who would not miss a chance for backbiting his colleague or immediate boss to the higher authority. So his answer is ready to the expected query from Governor, "Where is the Deputy Governor?" "He is so much amused... etc." This small touch adequately brings out the man, his personal ambition, his pettiness, meanness. He is a Governor out and out. So he would tactfully use the Deputy's sympathy for Ranjan as a handle against him and take this chance to further his own ambition.

Deputy Governor

The Assistant Governor's shrewd and mean undercutting of the Deputy helps us to understand the Deputy's nature and the man's temperamental difference from the other governors/rulers.

> He is so much amused by this fellow that he doesn't want to lay hands on him. He says the man's laugh shows what queer creatures we governors have grown into. (30)

That he can still respond to the charm of Ranjan shows his humanity has not yet withered up like the rest of the ruling coterie.

As soon as the Deputy Governor enters the stage one has the impression that he is somewhat different from the rest of the rulers. While entering he announces he has 'just sent' the dancing girls and musicians to the garden, where the rulers' families will join a feast. Governor asks him conspiratorially about "that little matter about Ranjan". The following dialogue brings out the man's character in relief against the unmitigated cynical cruelty of Governor; at the same time it sheds light on Governor, Headman and Assistant Governor who can sink to any level of sadism and even enjoy it; furthermore, it discloses in grim flashes the kind of detestable conspiracy that is executed by these men—unspoken things, as indicated by the hyphens, make the terror only the more horrifying:

> *Deputy Governor.* That kind of work is not in my line. The Assistant Governor has taken it upon himself to do the job. By this time his—
>
> *Governor.* Does the King—?
>
> *Deputy Governor.* The King can't possibly have understood. Some lie told by our men has goaded Ranjan to frenzy, and he's rushing to the usual fate of—*I detest the whole business.* Moreover, I don't think it right to deceive the King like this.
>
> *Governor.* That responsibility is mine. Now then, that girl must be—
>
> *Deputy Governor.* Don't talk of all that to me. The Headman who has been put on duty is the right man,—he doesn't shrink at any dirtiness whatever. (43; emphasis added)

Perhaps he would have been happy if he could dissociate himself from these criminal plans; but cannot, possibly because he is not a challenging rebel but only an escapist who wants to be exempted from an unpleasant job. Governor has rightly sized him up: "My friend, I see the instinct of the Ruler doesn't seem to match with the colour of your own blood..." and the Deputy replies with caustic bitterness, which is directed more at himself than the addressee, "There's hope still. Human blood is fast drying up" (43). Is he also a trapped man, waiting for the worst tragedy, the tragedy of dehumanization of self? No wonder, this schismatic person 'can't stomach' No. 321, i.e. the Headman. One wonders why did Tagore introduce such varied shades of personalities as counterpoints within the counterpoint?

Headman

The Headman is an example of unmixed servile evil. He is one of the henchmen of the system, the Governor's own team —who keep the machine of an oppressive system oiled and rolling.

With their brief appearance on the stage these small people leave a distinct impression upon the spectator. As Governor entrusts him with a 'duty' which is in no way official—to help his wife changing post near the Headman's village—he is disgustingly eager to oblige: "There is a plague on the cattle of our parish, and not a single ox can be had to draw the car. Never mind, we can press the diggers into service" (40). The suggestion brings out in a sudden grim flash the rulers' dehumanizing attitude and treatment of the diggers. Indeed, these crude henchmen of brutal power have no qualms in treating fellow humans as beasts, dragging them along the road, chained like a beast; as Bishu, under arrest, says fearlessly: "They have a big beast inside them, that's why their heads are not lowered by the indignity of man, rather the inner brute's tail swells and wags with pride at man's downfall" (39).

And all the time Headman is busy promoting some personal interest or undermining another's security, the typical reptilian creature fawning on the vestige of the powerful, a quite familiar figure to all of us. Governor makes no attempt to conceal his contempt, but the base creature does not mind. The Deputy Governor's estimate of the Headman throws adequate light on the latter's baseness,—"he doesn't stick at any dirtiness whatever" (43). It is with the eager service of such people that an oppressive system thrives.

Doctor

Doctor is another small but useful spoke in this wheel of unholy power. Like the religious man the medical man too prostitutes his vocation in the service of the system. He does not work towards curing illness and saving human life; his role is to preserve the bodies so as to provide the necessary work-force. He works at the instance of Governor, apparently he is Governor's instrument towards keeping a man "as much alive as it is necessary for him to be" (36); Governor does not trust the king; therefore, he has employed Doctor as a spy to keep watch upon the king. From his brief conspiratorial exchange with Governor, "I've seen him. I find the King" (40), one has a wiry hunch that these people are hatching some plan against the King.

Professor

The Professor is an intellectual by profession, whose intellect has been surrendered in the service of the system of the Yakshapuri. Yet he is not like the Doctor. In a way, Professor is also a digger as Nandini perceives: 'You who burrow day and night in a mass of yellow pages, like your diggers in the bowels of the earth' (4). Even so, he has not been completely eclipsed by it like Governor, Gosain or Doctor. This becomes apparent when we notice his response to Nandini, which reflects a kind of honest surprise. He first appears on the stage while addressing Nandini:

> Why do you come and startle one, now and again, and then pass by? Since you awaken a cry in our hearts, what harm if you stop a moment in answer to it? Let us talk a little. (4)

In answer to Nandini's question why he wonders at her, the Professor explains: "The sunlight gleaming through the forest thickets surprises nobody, but the light that breaks through a cracked wall is quite a different thing. In Yaksha Town, you are this light that startles..." (4). The Professor explains to the Antiquarian, who is a newcomer in the place, and as yet not quite conversant with its ways:

> She has for her mantle the green joy of the earth. That is our Nandini. In this Yaksha Town there are governors, headmen, tunnel-diggers, scholars like myself; there are policemen, executioners, and undertakers,—altogether a beautiful assortment! Only *she* is out of element. Midst the clamour of the market place she is a tuned-up lyre. (31)

He further admits how he is distracted by this phenomenon called Nandini: "There are days when the mesh of my studies is torn by the sudden breeze of her passing by, and through that rent my attention flies away swish, like a bird" (31).

The Professor seems to speak in the slightly mocking tone of a benign grandfather. Yet there is also a hidden resentful, bitterness which bursts through the seams of his apparently pleasant talk, though his oblique critique is presented in the garb of humor, it is nevertheless an acid humor. As Nandini says, it puzzles her to see a whole city thrusting its head underground, groping for dead wealth, the Professor explains, smilingly of course, though his words are dripping bitterness: "The *Jinn* of that dead wealth we invoke. If we can enslave him the whole world lies at our feet", and adds like a rejoinder, "As the ghost of our dead wealth is fearfully potent so is our ghostly royalty, made hazy by this net, with its inhuman power to frighten people" (4).

This is his way of protesting against the way of life in Yaksha Town. The sharpness of his mind flashes up at moments, as in his quick repartee to Nandini's charge that all he says is "a kind of made-up talk": "Of course made-up. The naked is without a credential, it's the made-up clothes that define us" (4). But sometimes he can barely retain the mask of humor, and a tragic seriousness casts shadow, as he says, "Yaksha Town is a city under eclipse"; or wonders why should the girl pick up the oleander from all flowers for her ornament, "Do you know we often choose our own fate thus, without knowing it!" (6).

Professor represents the typical confusion and conflict of the elite in this society. He is simultaneously attracted and repulsed by the system. Yet secretly in his innermost heart there is hope for a 'time': "When the time comes for showing us out, the great ones themselves will point the way..." (33). To Nandini's question, "Does it at all make for their well-being thus to keep watch and ward over these man-traps night and day?", Professor makes his sardonic comment: "Well-being! There's no question of 'well' in it at all—only 'being'. That *being* of theirs has expanded so terribly that, unless millions of men are pressed into service, who's going to support its weight.... They must exist, you see" (34). We come to know that he had 'told' (friendly warning?) Gajju at the outset that no 'show of heroics' will be allowed here for a moment, whereas Governor had provoked the wrestler into the encounter and thus crushed him.

Thus Professor appears to have retained at least some humanity in spite of the dehumanization all around; therefore, it does not seem unexpected or anachronistic when at the end the elderly man too leaves his cell and joins the diggers in their onward march to pull down the prison.

The Commoners

(i) Ordinary

Sometimes it has been wrongly assumed that Tagore could not perceive or portray commoners. The novels and the plays bear ample evidence to Tagore's power of observation—sometimes amused, sometimes compassionate—which is often brought out by means of sharp flashes, and minute cute touches of a casual stroke of brush.

Phagulal and Chandra

Phagulal and Chandra, the digger couple, represent the countless disempowered commoners, victims of the establishment in Yaksha Town. Though they have become accustomed to the place they still feel a kind of longing for the home village they had left behind for coming here. During the harvest season they want to go home. But they have been made distinct individuals with very different responses to people and things; whereas Phagulal is stirred by Nandini's vibrancy and ultimately he will follow Nandini to join the rebels, Chandra is jealous of her. Chandra is an instance of the very real portraits of common men and women that Tagore could do so effectively with just a few brush-strokes. She is vivid with her petty jealousy and limited vision. With her limited mind she fails to summon any sympathy for the girl, and mentions her as witch instead. As Bishu enters absorbed in his own song, she comments:

> He's been possessed by Nandini.... The witch is up to all kinds of tricks, and is sure to bring misfortune. (12)

A little later she adds:

> To see her flaunting her prettiness all over the place makes me sick. (12)

Chandra, again, is easily won over by the priest's hypocritical oratory, whereas Phagulal can see through him. Incidentally, Chandra is also taken in by Governor's artificial smile, by the 'gorgeous array' of the procession of Governors and their wives on the occasion of Flag worship.

Gokul

Tagore never draws his world in black-and-white. Though the diggers are victims of the system, individually they are not all angels. Gokul is a digger who has been vividly individualized with just a few brush-strokes. He is rude, sadist and suspicious by nature. Tagore is adept in doing such small people with their habitual meanness and limitations. For instance, one can recall the long pageant of ordinary people in *Gorā*—from Baradasundari to Harimohini, from Kailash to Mahim, from Krishnadayal to Haranbabu, from Mahim's wife to Labanya, and from the reptilian Madhab Chatterjee to the vulturish police inspector, the arrogant magistrate Brownlow, the brute policemen—amusingly/revoltingly small and mean. They are, however, no less vivacious and entertaining. These flashes adequately show that Tagore could be as realistic as any of the valorized realistic writers (Saratchandra, for instance); like Gulliver holding the Liliputians on his palm, Tagore could at ease pick these small people up for instantaneous playful observation and then leave them indifferently on the roadside to go ahead with his main characters.

Gokul is by nature suspicious, a potential sadist, given to spurts of violence. He is by temperament inclined to faultfinding with others. One can imagine him talking in loud metallic voice. Gokul is a very limited person, and he wants to understand a thing clearly in his own limited way; he is suspicious of what he fails to understand, and his failure makes him aggressive towards the object. "I don't trust what I can't understand", he says in so many words; hence his aggressive rudeness towards Nandini, whom he cannot understand.

Like Chandra, Gokul too thinks of her suspiciously as a witch. Although Chandra's motivation is jealousy, Gokul is prompted by fear of what he, in his blunt insensitivity, fails to grasp. Even Gokul, who has been dehumanized under the system, feels a kind of uneasiness at the presence of Nandini. Gokul cannot understand her, therefore cannot trust her either. He is like the blunt fascist activist/muscleman of an autocratic political party. He bluntly confronts Nandini:

> *Gokul.* Turn this way, woman! Who are you? I've never yet been able to understand you....

I don't trust what I can't understand....

....

I don't believe you, one bit!...Oh, you terrible, terrible witch! (7)

At the same time Gokul also feels a strange attraction, though this attraction only stirs up fear and violence within him: "You know some spell, I'm sure. You're snaring everybody here. You're a witch! Those who are bewitched by your beauty will come to their death" (7). Towards the end this innate violence finds its grim expression as Gokul is about to hack her with his heavy club.

At the end when all are set, including the King, for breaking the prison Gokul and Chandra are found missing. Phagulal says: "She has gone with her tears and prayers to the Governor, accompanied by Gokul. I am afraid Gokul is seeking to take up service with the Governor. He will betray us" (49). Perhaps this would have been the right placement for people like Gokul all along; persons like Chandra, with their limited minds, readily fall for them.

The Commoners

(ii) Extraordinary

Kishor

Kishor and Bishu, both slaves of the system, yet represent an extraordinary spirit of resilience, which they achieve through love. Kishor is a very young digger who has not been here long. Kishor is not only the name. He is Kishor in age too; so he can speak of his feelings without hesitation. Kishor epitomizes the pure innocence of a boy; so he can recognize beauty and also respond to it spontaneously without inhibition. He intuitively knows beauty and its worth. Kishor has no greed for the dough of gold.

Because the Yaksha Town has not yet swallowed him up, he can turn to Nandini with the love of his eager innocent mind; it is owing to this love that he procures red oleanders for her at considerable risk. The play starts with Kishor, excitedly entering the stage; he is excited at discovering a plant of red oleanders. He is happy that the flowers, which Nandini said she must have, are not easily available in this place. He tells Nandini: "I am glad they're hard to find in this place".

He does not fear or worry about punishment; that means physical pain does not affect his mind.

Nandini. But it breaks my heart to know that those brutes punish you.

Kishor. It makes these flowers all the more preciously mine. They come from my pain. (3)

Again, in a later scene, when Bishu is led in chains Kishor wants to persuade the guards to take him in exchange: "Punishment won't hurt me. I am young. I shall bear it with joy" (39). Significantly, it is Kishor, a mere boy, who is assigned the "dangerous work" (39)—the challenging task of finding out Ranjan in this huge Gulag. It is adolescence which is sent to search out endangered youth. And Kishor dies while carrying out the mission; but prior to death he has done his duty—he has handed over the bunch of red oleanders to Ranjan. This is what he had dreamt of as he said to Nandini on his first appearance: "I dream of dying one day for your sake" (3). This avowal flashes upon Nandini as she notices the flower in the dead hand of Ranjan. As she challenges, the King informs, Kishor has disappeared like a bubble, because the poor boy, with a woman's charming face and strange haughty words, had dared to take on the King. "He burst himself against me, like a bubble" (48).

Kishor can be placed in line with Uttiya in Tagore's dance-drama *Shyāmā*, who is mentioned as *bālak kiśôr* (*a young boy*), and who sacrifices his life for the sake of the woman he loves; or Amulya in *Ghare-Bāire* (*The Home and the World*), the teenage boy who takes great risk to help Bimala, whom he adores. The innocence and nobility of this selfless love of a boy for an older woman recurs in Tagore's oeuvre as a repeated motif, which can be examined from the perspective of psychological criticism.

Bishu

Bishu is called Bishu the madcap—derisively by some, lovingly by Nandini. There had been a time when Bishu was part of this autocratic establishment. But eventually he was got rid of. Now he is a misfit in the Yaksha Town, and generally passes off as the mad one. This is again a recurring feature of Tagore's plays; a madman, or a grandpa, or a Baul singer,—somebody outside the pale of the common run of life, and thereby lending a special dimension and perspective to the play. Bishu is to Nandini what Dhananjoy Bairagi is to the Prince Abhihit in *Free Water*—a musical inspiration and support. In answer to the King's anxious and annoyed query, "Nandini, what is this man to you?", she replies: "He's my partner in music. My heart soars in his voice, my pain cries in his tunes, that's what he tells me" (25). Indeed, the 'partnership' between Nandini and Bishu, a long-lost and recently found friend, has touched a special altitude. Whereas Kishor supplies flowers Bishu brings his gift of songs for Nandini.

Bishu had started work in Yaksha Town with the job of a spy for the establishment. It was a 'comfortable job' by any standard, but he could not stick to it, and eventually gave up. But he cannot break away from the place. It is apparent that Bishu is not liked much by the Governor, who holds him in suspicion, and naturally. He is certainly intriguing for this man who cannot make out why the man rejected position and status (his wife used to receive calls for joining the Governors' wives at their card-game) and chose to come down among the diggers instead; a shrewd materialistic mind cannot but conclude that he has some design up his sleeves.

Obviously Bishu is not an average digger; he has a depth of mind, a sweet disposition, and above all a sensitive decent mind which retains the capacity to soar. Nandini says, "In this closed fort a bit of sky survives only between you and me..." (20). He has looked into his own heart and has known, "The pain of desire for the near belongs to the animal, the sorrow of aspiration for the far belongs to man. That far away flame of my eternal sorrow is revealed through Nandini" (20). If Ranjan is joy, Bishu is sorrow. Joy and sorrow together make life rich. He is the obverse side of Ranjan. Seeing Bishu by Nandini's side the King's voice asks brusquely: "Who is that with you? A pair to Ranjan?" Bishu steps forward to reply: "No, King, I am the obverse side of Ranjan, on which falls the shadow" (25). When

Chandra asks Bishu, "Tell me, Bishu, what does she charm you with?", Bishu says, "The charm of sorrow", and then further explains: "She reminds me that there are sorrows, to forget which is the greatest sorrow" (20). It is "the charm of sorrow" (20) that binds him to Nandini. In one of his songs he addresses Nandini as 'O waker of my grief!' (21). Through the dialog between Nandini and Bishu we can guess they knew each other before coming to the place, possibly Bishu loved her, but did not stake his claim; subsequently, he was brought to Yaksha Town by 'a woman', like a bird brought to the dust by a chance arrow. Yet Bishu has no anger or resentment against his wife as he mentions the event.

Before Nandini came to this place Bishu just maintained the average digger's life, although his refusal to do the job of spying was a way of protest. But as a digger he maintained a low profile so that the Governor spared him "out of sheer contempt". But with the arrival of Nandini, and their renewed friendship, Bishu gets over his fear by degrees. He explains the change: "I felt as if they had pounded me.... Then you came and looked into my face in a way that made me sure some light could still be seen through me" (20). He tells Nandini, "when I am with you my mind scorns to be cautious" (24). The proof follows immediately; in reply to the Governor's query about the subject of his talk he says point-blank, "We are discussing how to escape from this fortress of yours". The Governor can barely hide his astonishment: "Really? So recklessly, that you don't even mind confessing it?" (24). Towards the end, after being arrested for "speaking out the truth...at last", Bishu says, "at last I am free" (38), "these chains will bear witness to the truth of my freedom" (39).

No Children

Children frequently figure in Tagore's plays and take dominant roles. Here, however, Tagore has carefully kept children out of his dramatic space, but the presence of couples is indicated—Phagulal-Chandra, Bishu-his wife, the governors and their wives. Why? Is it because the environment is so dead and cruel that children would have been misfits here, and it would have been too cruel to bring them into the dark arena of the Yaksha Town, in the suffocating grim concentration camp where trigger-happy guards come down upon bent-backed people in chains forced to dig in darkness for dead gold?

Technique

(i) Pālā

Tagore himself described the play as *Pālā*—a popular folk form of theatre in India. Pala is usually based upon some very well-known legendary story—outline. *Pālā* means the oral/ written text/script of *Jatra*, a traditional and very popular form of folk theatre in Bengal. *Pālā* also means a long narrative—usually unsophisticated, and drawing from a common pool of public memory for its subject—either sung or performed on stage with a lot of songs and dances—both being of folk-origin.

At the same time Tagore makes a most fine use of symbols which were of course not the way of the age-old *Pālā*. Tagore in this play shows an interesting twining of the ancient folk-form with *avante-garde* dramaturgy.

(ii) Symbols

(a) *Gold*

Tagore wrote in the Preface to the play: "that agriculture has forgotten itself under the pull of a demonic avarice—in order to convey this message in a covert manner in the *Tretāyug* the magical gold deer had been introduced. Isn't it the lure of the magical gold deer of the Rakshasa that the Sitas of today fall easy prey to the demon; otherwise why should the peasants abandon their villages under the cool shadow of the big sprawling trees to embrace the deadly life at the Titagarh jute mills? All these came about in later times than Valmiki's..." (my translation).

Shambhu Mitra interprets this as not mineral gold "just as Hanuman too did not burn down a Lanka of mineral gold"; he would rather hold it as the "fossil fuel, which the earth had kept buried for long ages", and further argues, "this thoughtless greedy use of natural resources is a major feature of this machine age" (Mitra 27; my translation).

There are also hints of another kind of gold; this is conveyed through the music that wafts in at intervals from the distant fields. While the diggers of the Yaksha Town are delving deep into the bowels of the earth, and coming up with heaps of gold, music resonates across the fields far away—music about the gold of sunlight spreading over the earth, a music that stirs in the diggers a longing for their village home in the lap of open nature, so much that they even think of asking for leave to go home.

Two kinds of gold are counterpoised through the text: the dead gold on the one hand, and on the other the gold of life gleaming in the light of the sun, the colour of the ripe corn, the beauty of Nandini. The dead wealth of tangible gold is associated with darkness, with the underworld which is the mythic domain of death, whereas the epitomes of intangible gold belong to the realm of light and life. Early in the play the Professor highlights this counterpoint as he tells Nandini:

> In this Yaksha Town all our treasure is of gold, the secret treasure of the dust. But the gold which is you, beautiful one, is not of the dust, but of the light which never owns any bond. (4)

Perhaps that is why this gold fails to attract Nandini. Nandini makes it clear to the King, that her admiration for the King is not stirred by his gold, but by his strength with which he handles the gold. She unambiguously points the lack, the dearth in this dead treasure:

> The day you let me into your store-house the blocks of gold did not surprise me,—what amazed me was the immense strength with which you lifted and arranged them. But can blocks of gold ever answer to the swinging rhythm of your arms in the same way as fields of corn? (8)

Then she asks the King, "Are you not afraid, King, of handling the dead wealth of the earth?" She explains the 'fear': "The living heart of the earth gives itself up in love and life and beauty, but when you rend its bosom and disturb the dead, you bring up with your booty the curse of its dark demon, blind and hard, cruel and envious. Don't you see everybody here is either angry, or suspicious, or afraid?" (8).

The gold is not a thing of necessity for the King, but it is obsession; Bishu says, in conclusion to his penetrating discourse on drink: "These nuggets are the drink—the solid drink—of our Gold King" (15). Still the dead weight of amassed gold cannot yield one facet of a touchstone. Even as the play opens, the King has already begun to realize that all he possesses is only "so much dead weight. No increase of gold can create a particle of a touchstone" (9).

The symbol of gold also tangentially foregrounds several counterpoints as follows:

1. The 'dead' gold and the golden light of the autumnal sun; the gold of the ripe corn-sheaf.
2. The deadly power of gold and the vibrant youth of Ranjan.
3. "The stolen wine of the prison house", the "wine of death" in Bishu's song, which "flushes all emptiness with laughter" (13), and the "boundless tavern, underneath the blue canopy". (13)
4. The dark tunnels leading to the dark mines underground and the open corn-fields flooded with sunlight.
5. The golden spires of the palace and the sunset clouds. Bishu describes how he had drifted to Yaksha Town in terms of contrapuntal images of gold which highlights his basic difference from his wife.

   "One day, while I was gazing at the sunset clouds, she had her eye upon the golden spire of the Governor's palace. Her glance challenged me to take her over there. In my foolish pride I vowed to do so. When I did bring her here, under the golden spire, the spell was broken." (22)

6. Diggers and Tillers; Nandini charges the Professor as another 'digger' into dead things.

(b) *The Iron Net*

The King remains invisible behind a net. The Antiquarian, new to the place, is stunned by the information, "There's no means of meeting him. You'll have to talk to him from outside this network" (31).

The play opens with the direction: "The curtain rises on a window covered by a network of intricate pattern in front of the Palace." In parenthetic stage direction it is denoted as a window—(Nandini [knocking at the window]. Do you hear?...) (25), and also mentioned just as 'network'—(Nandini [shaking the network violently]. Open the door…) (47).

It is across this netting that the dialog between Nandini and the King is carried on. Nandini implores him to come out from behind the net: "come out into the light, step on the ground, let the earth be glad" (8). But the King fails to respond.

Tagore mentions this as "cover of an intricate network—the scientific system".

> It is an organized passion of greed that is stalking abroad in the name of European civilization.… Such an objectified passion lacks the true majesty of human nature; it only assumes a terrifying bigness, its physiognomy blurred through its cover of an intricate net-work,—the scientific system. It barricades itself against all direct human touch with barriers of race pride and prestige of power.

Nandini asks Professor: "…you hide your King behind a wall of netting. Is it for fear of people finding out that he's a man?" (4). Professor answers in his characteristic tone of mild mockery: "As the ghost of our dead wealth is fearfully potent so is our ghostly royalty, made hazy by this net, with its inhuman power to frighten people" (4). At a climactic moment in the play Nandini desperately knocks and pushes at the network, crying, "Listen, listen, listen!" Gosain asks, with his typical touch of sardonic vulgarity, whom is she 'prodding' like that; Nandini bursts out: "That boa-constrictor of yours, who remains in hiding and swallows men" (44). It is only towards the end that the King comes out of his net to join his own rebellious people (47).

Does the net signify a convenient device installed and maintained by the Governors who run the place in the name of the King? So that the 'Big Brother' (*à la* Orwell) remains inaccessible to common people, so that the common individuals can establish no connection with him, the King has been kept separated from the rest behind a net. It is also deliberately meant to create confusion, like a mist; during a moment of exasperation Nandini says, "That King of yours, shrouded in his mist of netting." It is the obstacle put up to preclude communication, as well as clarity.

The net suggests the inaccessibility and abstraction of modern power as well as "the panoptic modality of power" (*à la* Foucault 211) at all levels; one can find a correspondence to this idea in Foucault's argument: "The state is superstructural in relation to a whole series of networks...these networks stand in a conditioning-conditioned relationship to a kind of 'metapower' which is structured essentially around a certain number of great prohibition functions" (Foucault 64). The network in the play is an instrument in the hands of the oppressors; the net serves their vested interest. Therefore the net can be ever-spreading instead of being a fixed size and shape. Its scope can be all-encompassing like the power of a totalitarian state. To Nandini's agonized question at seeing the torture perpetrated upon her village neighbors, Professor says: "Well-being! There's no question of 'well' in it at all,—only 'being'. That *being* of theirs has expanded so terribly that, unless millions of men are pressed into service, who's going to support its weight? So *the net is spreading farther and farther*" (34; emphasis added), in order to ensure their existence. The netted window thus also becomes a paradigm for the entire place which is but an extended and inescapable concentration camp, a paradigm for the entire system which is an all-pervasive and all-powerful labyrinthine prison, an epitome of what Foucault calls "the regular extension, the infinitely minute web of panoptic techniques" (Foucault 213). The Professor's comment on the Antiquarian's futile attempt at escaping Yaksha Town sends a shudder down the spine:

> You see how our Antiquarian has quietly slipped off, thinking he'll fly and save himself. After going a few steps, he'll soon discover that there's a wire network stretched from post to post, from country to country. (33-34)

Again, the net in front of the King seems to guard an exclusive and exclusivist space behind it. Thus it becomes a net within the net, as it were. The King says he wants to see Nandini and Ranjan together. Nandini points out the hindrance to 'see'-ing : "You won't be able to see from behind your net" (25). The 'Voice' says, "I shall let you sit inside my room", simply because he wants to 'know' them. Once one is allowed inside the net, one becomes the object, and ceases to be the subject of the sentence—object of voyeurism, of 'knowing'—that is mechanical analysis, and at the worst—of torture and annihilation. However, the one occasion on which Nandini had been allowed inside, the King did not try to 'know', but surrendered to the moment instead, and so Nandini did not find the King fearsome there, he appeared rather like some great mythical type instead.

But this must have been a very rare moment; significantly this has not been presented, but only reported instead. Otherwise the King remains a mysterious disembodied 'Voice', invisible, inaccessible, and frequently intractable in his own exclusive space behind the net, which continues to send hints of a terrible operation going on inside. Once, from behind the net the King throws a dead frog outside; later we find dead/squeezed humans (the left-over of the King) being churned out.

Seen from the perspective of Tagore's dramatic oeuvre, the net can call up a cluster of associated symbols, like the solid wall of *Acalāyatan*, or the dam of *Free Water*. Like the wall symbolizing the stagnated mind of man, or the dam metaphorizing the force that stops the flow of love, the net too semiotizes the imprisonment of dynamic living energy which has been made inert by some deadening mechanical power.

Bhattacharya draws attention to a running motif in Tagore's symbolic-allegoric plays: it is the stagnation/ entrapment/imprisonment of the human soul and his subsequent release from the obstruction. The net can also be considered in this light. The obstacle can come from within, or be posed from outside; through the blinding ego of man, or through obscurantist constraining systems of society/religion. Thus Sudarsana (*Rājā*) is entrapped by her addiction to external beauty and desire; Mahapanchak (*Acalāyan*) is confined within the prison of obscurantist, ritualistic religion; Amal (*Post-Office*) is kept imprisoned by scriptural strictures, by society, by family; the King (*Fālguṇī*) is entrapped by his own lust and fear of senility; King Ranajit (*Muktadhārā*) is obsessed by the power of science and the lust for imperial power.

In line with the above, the King in *Red Oleanders* is imprisoned by his own avarice for unlimited wealth, his pride of material power, and the mechanical system he has installed. The net symbolizes this imprisonment. Though it seems self-opted, yet it is also obsessive for him. It is only at the end when he can realize his mistake that he can come out from behind this net. But in course of the play the 'Voice' behind the net grows increasingly fretful, and Nandini wonders, "It is you who entangle yourself in your own net, then why keep on fretting?" (220). Ultimately in the clash between the iron net and the red oleander flower, paradoxically it is the flower that wins, while the net collapses.

On one occasion the Professor admits his own scholarship to be a 'net' of defence behind which he hides like the King hiding behind his own net. "Do you know Nandini", he says, "I too live behind a net-work of scholarship. I am an unmitigated scholar just as our King is an unmitigated king." (5). Of course he seems to say this in an unmistakable tone of self-mockery.

(c) *The Frog*

On one occasion, the King, from behind the invisibility of the network, stretches out his hand and drops a dead frog outside, on the stage. Nandini shudders. The Voice rolls on in monotone (presumably):

> Once upon a time this frog got into a hole in a stone, and in that shelter it existed for three hundred years. I have learnt from it the secret of continuing to exist, but to live it does not know. To-day I felt bored and smashed its shelter. I've thus saved it from existing forever. Isn't that good news? (25)

The petty and unpleasant detail acquires symbolic dimension in the context of the basic counterpoint posed by the play between non-living and living, death-in-life existence and buoyant vibrancy of real life; this also carries a hint of the King's grim search for power and his boredom with the same, which gives a clue to his growing restiveness.

(d) *The Floral Symbol: /Title: /Signifier[Signiflower]*

Tagore said he would refuse to take the responsibility for any debacle that might be caused by the critics' search for meaning supposed to have lain hidden between the petals of the flower. Yet the flower, mention of which lies interspersed through the text, and which constitutes the very title, indeed emerges as a loaded image in the course of the play, which was first titled as *Yakshapuri*, then it was changed to *Nandini* and finally *Nandini* was replaced by *Raktakarabi*.

The very opening is signaled by a bunch of the flower,—as Kishor rushes in with some red oleander flowers, excited at his success in getting them at considerable personal risk. Just because Nandini said, she "*must* have red oleanders" Kishor has staked a lot to gather it; he is 'glad' that "they're hard to find in this place", because that poses a challenge for him. "Only one tree I discovered after days of search, nearly hidden away behind a rubbish heap". Incidentally, Kishor's description of the location of the plant closely corresponds to a personal experience of the author. Pramathanath Bishi cites from a letter, written to him by Pandit Kshitimohan Senshastri, in which Senshastri refers to Tagore's mention of the flowers in the play just a few days prior to his death "Close to my room there was a garbage heap of scrap iron things. A small Karabi sapling had been buried under it. When it first fell under the garbage I did not notice; afterwards the scraps were removed but the little sapling could not be traced. After a certain time suddenly one day I caught the sight of a delicate graceful Karabi-branch had sprung up above the iron rubbish, holding one red flower in its bosom. As if showing its heart's blood spouting up at a cruel blow, it came to greet lovingly with sweet smile. It said, "See, I didn't die! You couldn't nip me, could you?" This revelation then stirred my mind with pain. Prior to this I had entitled the play variously as 'Yakshapuri', 'Nandini', etc, but I was not happy with any of these names; so now I conferred it the name, 'Raktakarabi'" (my translation). In the play too there is only one plant of Raktakarabi (Red Oleander), and that has come up untended, unnoticed, by the garbage heap at one end of the Yakshapuri. Indeed the system of the Yakshapuri is not supposed to accommodate flower shrubs.

For Kishor the flowers are 'preciously' his own, because, as he claims, "they come from my pain"; he has to gather the flowers with great difficulty and at considerable risk. Thus from the very start the flower ceases to be a mere flower, and in course of the play becomes increasingly a signifier. For Kishor the flowers are his 'homage' to Nandini, and in the bitter ignominy of his life in Yaksha Town at last he has found a 'triumph', that has made him bold. To Nandini's anxious admonition, he says, "No, no, I shall be rash and defy their blows. My homage shall be my daily triumph."

On the other hand, the Professor who yearns for one flower in the garland Nandini is weaving, lets out his uneasy intuition about her floral choice in an unguarded moment: "How often have I thought that there is some omen in these ornaments of yours." As Nandini says she knows no omen, the Professor murmurs in a serious note of apprehension: "Perhaps your fate knows. In that red there is not only beauty, but also the fascination of fear." It is interesting that the very same flower which inspires Bishu to defy 'fear', stirs the Professor to respond to 'the fascination of fear'; he wonders why the girl opted for this particular flower in preference to all others. So he mutters almost to himself, "I don't know what event you have come to write with that crimson tint", and adds, "Do you know, we often choose our own fate thus, without knowing it!" (6). Nandini explains her preference in romantic articulation. "Ranjan sometimes calls me Red Oleander. I feel that the colour of his love is red,—that red I wear on my neck, on my breast, on my arms" (6). [Incidentally, allusions to the scarlet or vermilion of spring flowers run through the countless spring songs and poems of Tagore; for instance, his famous spring song, "Oh, look there, Spring has burst out like a red fire in the forests".] Professor would beg for "just one of those flowers" from her, though in the same breath he adds in a tone of self-mockery: "let me try to understand the meaning of its colour" (6); as if he remembers his limitation. To the Professor's cool, cynical wisdom, the flowers are a sign of desperate defiance which is bound to be futile, howsoever charming it may look. So he tries to play down, albeit with a barely suppressed sadness, Nandini's honest anger against the crushing system as "the wild cry of red oleander" (35). In his perception by degrees Nandini becomes identified with the flowers which belong to the realm of light and air, in contrast to the dark underground which rules life here; hence his appeal to her: "My sweet Red Oleander, don't try to probe our secrets in the depths of their dust. Be for us swaying in the air above, that we may gaze upwards to see you" (36). Through this half-serious appeal Professor actually makes a semiotic gesture in which Nandini gets merged with the flower.

The habitually suspicious Gokul on the other hand, who does not trust what he cannot understand, must have the 'meaning' of the 'dangling' thing over her forehead; Nandini's indifferent answer that it has no meaning, sends him into a frenzy of fear, so much that he abuses her as a 'terrible witch' and an 'ominous torch'. Thus for Gokul also the flower presents a sign—the sign of the 'ominous torch' indicating a dangerous witch.

The King, at another level, feels no less uneasy about the soft petals which he cannot possess. "Why can't I strain out the tint of your oleanders and build a dream out of it to keep before my eyes? Those few frail petals guard it and hinder me" (8). But not even the King can have them, since Nandini's oleander flowers are exclusively meant for Ranjan. The King's complex attitude of mistrust and longing, jealousy and love is foregrounded by his ambivalent response of synchronic longing and violence regarding the flowers. So he would angrily turn out Nandini, and immediately implore her, "No, no, wait a little. Give me that tassel of red oleanders which hangs from your hair." Yet when Nandini asks what he would do with it, he says:

> When I look at those flowers it seems to me as if the red light of my evil star has appeared in their shape. At times I want to snatch them from you and tear them to

pieces. Again I think that if Nandini were ever to place that spray of flowers on my head, with her own hands, then—... Then perhaps I might die in peace.

Nandini. Some one loves red oleanders and calls me by that name. It is in remembrance of him that I wear these flowers.

Voice. Then, I tell you, they're going to be *his* evil star as well as *mine.* (26)

The flower thus serves as a motif to draw out the working of the troubled mind of a split personality which is curiously torn between the sadism of fierce possessiveness and the peace of loving surrender.

Towards the end when Kishor is sent by Bishu to find out Ranjan, Nandini hands over the 'tassel of red oleanders' from her hair (39). The flower thus again becomes a sign/code, her insignia, her encrypted eloquent message for Ranjan. Finally, at the end when all the workers and prisoners are rushing out to join the fight with the Governor's force, Phagulal notices something: "Here is her wristlet of red oleanders. She has bared her arm today,—and left us." Bishu bends low and tenderly picks it up in a gesture of great sorrow, great humility: "Once I told her I would not take anything from her hand. I break my word and take this. Come along!" With their departure the play ends while the music of autumn reverberates in the distance.

The bunch of red oleander flowers can be considered the floral symbol of what Nandini manifests as a human figure. The flower is a pure imagistic form of what Nandini is in actuality. According to Bishi, Nandini is the essence of life's vibrancy; the flower is the essence of Nandini. It is Nandini in abstraction, isolated from specific, circumstantial detail, evoking the irrepressible power of life above all forces of death. Like Nandini the flower too bursts out amidst all-round repression, and springs up like the fountain. It is the indomitable, undefeatable spirit of life which refuses to die.

Again, it is only Kishor, a boy in his teens, who knows its location. He has recognized the essence of Nandini through his loving vision; perhaps that is why the flower has revealed its presence only to the boy.

The oleander finally denotes a vision of hope. In the letter of Senshastri to Bishi (mentioned earlier) we find, Tagore said: "Have no worry about life. The *Upanisad* says life is the true thing, it has no death; so the fear was for the inorganic. Now science claims, a thing made by nature also has no death. What die are the man-made artificial, untrue things. I have said this in *Raktakarabī*. Who has ever succeeded in killing life, even after tying it up with a thousand shackles, burying it over hundreds of times?" (trans. Present writer). At the end of the play we have a brief glimpse of Ranjan, lying dead, with the bunch of red oleanders on his bosom. As if he too is saying "See, I didn't die! You couldn't nip me, could you?". The flower symbolizes the irrepressible force of life which cannot be crushed, whose freedom cannot be robbed whatever bondage or shackles may have been applied to put it down. This is the subtext of the title.

The garland of red oleanders that Nandini makes is meant exclusively for Ranjan alone. At the same time there is mention of another flower, the white 'kunda'. Nandini offers a garland of white kunda flowers to Governor in return to his 'message of hope' that she will see Ranjan this very day. The Governor says, albeit sardonically, because he knows already his machinery for finishing Ranjan has been set in motion,— "Why throw away the garland thus, and not keep it for Ranjan?"

> *Nandini*. There is a garland for him.

Governor responds in a half-sardonic half-serious tone:

> *Governor*. Aha, I thought so! I suppose it's the one hanging round your neck. The garland of victory may be of *kunda* flowers, the gift of the hand; but the garland of welcome is of red oleanders, the gift of the heart. Well, let's be quick in accepting what comes from the hand, for that will fade; as for the heart's offering, the longer it waits the more precious it grows. (24)

Does the gift affect even the hardened man ever so slightly? At least he cannot resist being conscious of it; so the next time Nandini confronts him, he says, rather flippantly: "Hallo, Nandini, is that you? I shall wear your kunda chain late in the evening. When three-quarters of me can hardly be seen for the dark, then perchance a flower garland might become even me" (32). Again, on his re-entry, the first thing he mentions is the Gosain's surprise at seeing the garland in his room (36). Gosain, however, in tune with his mean nature, is suspicious of even this flower, but he hides his suspicion under the smooth garb of false velvet talks which still fail to hide the stink of vulgar pretence which is in his nature. "Ah indeed! The gift of a pure heart! God's own white *kunda* flowers! This is what gives one faith in the power of virtue, and hope for the sinners' redemption" (36). What right does he have to comment like this, with the air of a superior, on *her* gift to another? People like this assume the right to vulgarly interfere and control lives by means of glib hypocrisy. Thus the white flower draws out the blackness of the person.

At a climactic point towards the end the two flowers are thrown into a superb counterpoint; the King has already joined the rebels and the Governor is seen coming down with his soldiers. Nandini cries out: "He has swung up my garland of *kunda* flowers on his spear-head. I will dye that garland the colour of my oleanders with my heart's blood...Victory to Ranjan!" (50). Thus at this point the oleanders become synonym for the 'heart's blood', extreme daring, sacrifice, martyrdom, something like the 'rosa mystica' in Hopkins's poem, 'Rosa Mystica', which also shows the metamorphosis of a white rose into a red one through suffering and martyrdom. This is the last glimpse we get of Nandini, after which she rushes out, possibly to meet her death.

It seems interesting to note that both the flowers chosen by Nandini, red oleander as well as white kunda, are without fragrance. Why?

(iii) Music

Music has been frequently thematized in Tagore's plays through 'intermedial transposition' or 'intermedial reference'. Here music is 'contrapuntal' (*ā la* Said). The lost way of life close to nature, has been evoked at frequent intervals through intangible music floating in from some distance, or the impalpable nostalgic memory of the diggers; but this is never shown onstage.

(a) *The Harvesting Song*

The song of harvesting, which apparently wafts in, from distant fields, has been used as the 'prelude' and 'coda' in the play. This is the theme song. Sometimes it can be heard; sometimes it is inaudible, submerged under the harsh noise. Whenever there is a pause in the grinding, grating, rumbling sound of the machines of the Yaksha Town one can hear the song in the distance. But actually it is running through the space, the texture, the mood, and thus pervades the play, percolating through and seeping into every seam of the text, lending thereby to an additional thematic overtone as well as leading to an extraordinary aesthetic effect.

It is clearly a choric song, and not a solo one, although it is repeatedly made to overlap with Nandini's speech. The tune is very simple, like some folk-song, sung by common rural people. Nandini ignores Gokul's abusive speech as the song floats in.

> *Hark, 'tis Autumn calling:*
>
> *'Come, O come away!'—*
>
> *Her basket is heaped with corn.*

At this point Nandini speaks out, as if to herself, to any and everybody, including those in the audience, "Don't you see the September sun is spreading the glow of the ripening corn in the air?" (7).

During this utterance, we can imagine the music has not stopped, but continues in the distance; the moment she stops we can at once hear the song rising like the open wind over the fields.

> *Drunken with the perfumed wine of the wind,*
>
> *the sky seems to sway among the shivering corn,*
>
> *its sunlight trailing on the fields.*

Nandini calls out to the 'Voice' behind the net, "You too come out, King!—out into the fields" (7). All the while the song wafts in as the singers pass by in the distance. Again and again, at regular intervals the song, quite a part, or in snatches, can be heard rhythmically, sometimes coming closer, and sometimes receding in the distance until at the end it takes over.

While clearly indicating the season, the song, further, presents a counterpoint to the dead gold under the earth, by means of celebrating the golden sunlight rippling over the earth, embracing the golden ears of the ripe corn. Of course few here can hear the song. This music does not seem to reach the ears of the bulk of Yaksha Town population, who have imbibed the system heart and soul. The King cannot hear the song initially. When Nandini draws his attention he hears it at last, but he does not know what he would do in response, or if he could at all go out to the cornfields in case. Fagulal and Chandra can also hear the song, and they are visibly disturbed; they are pulled by a strong nostalgia for their lost village home and past.

The governors and the diggers do not hear the song. Even if it chances to reach their ears they would prefer to hold it out as an unnecessary nuisance. This insensitivity to the simple folk-song of harvest joys shows how alienated they have become from nature, its seasonal beauty, the ripe cornfield, its association of joy and pure abandon.

At the end we again hear the song in Bishu's voice:

Hark 'tis Autumn calling,—
Come, O come away!
The earth's mantle of dust is filled with ripe corn!
O the joy! the joy!

At this point the song seems to indicate a kind of fulfillment to be attained through sorrow, that the mantle of dust too is filled with golden corn; though the pity of the waste,—the ripe corn scattered on the dust, cannot be ignored either.

Shantikumar Dasgupta perceptively points out about the harvest song in *Red Oleanders* that it is the expression of the longing of all the people here who had been formerly tillers, but now reduced to numbers. Indeed, it is evocative of their yearning for the free, sunny, fulfilling life above the surface of the earth from under the dark-cramping-imprisoning life inside the bowel of the earth. It is the longing for the absent from the heart of the present. And the sadness emanating from that longing bursts forth through the song.

(b) *Other Songs*

Nandini sings an exuberant song, 'I love, I love'; but this annoys the king, and he disappears in the midst of the song, leaving a dead frog on the road under his window. Nandini guesses: "He is afraid of songs" (28).

Bishu sings several other songs to Nandini apart from his beautiful song addressed to his 'waker of grief' (21),—and the 'song of waiting' prior to the final catastrophe (29).

(c) *Latent Music*

Sambhu Mitra offers a finely sensitive discussion of the latent music in the play which, he feels, has been projected through the sequence of varied voices:

> ...I would like to draw attention to a special feature. The play is set off with the voice of a young boy, a fresh young voice. Next enters the voice of an elderly person. His scale is different. Next follows the metallic voice of Gokul. It is sound on a high pitch. Then comes the King's voice: 'Fields! What could I do there?'—a deep bass voice. And all the while Nandini's voice can be heard alongside. Four different relationships between Nandini and these four characters are expressed. Her instrument seems to play duet with four different instruments. It is like some wonderful orchestration. It is in this way that Rabindranath's musical talent has found expression in his play. When this orchestration is built up in course of acting, the spectators are not conscious as their attention has already been absorbed by the dialogue and characters. Yet through that very unconsciousness this musical artistry creates effect upon their senses. These are fine attributes of art.... (Mitra 25; my translation)

(d) *Anti-music*

The horrifying anti-music of Yaksha Town presents a contrast to the simple, charming song of the tillers in the field. The Antiquarian, a fresher to the place, is understandably shocked by this anti-music.

> *Antiquarian.* I say what is this infernal noise going on inside?
>
> ... It sounds like big pillars crashing down one after another. (31)

(iv) Dance rhythm

(a) *Rhythm of nature*

The King sees in Nandini his opposite, which he identifies as 'the dance rhythm' of the universe. Indeed Nandini is connected with the earth, the air, the light, from which the King has become disconnected. He does not know what he can do in the fields. Shambhu Mitra interprets this 'dance rhythm' as the rhythm of nature, its eco-system: that man must understand and follow the rhythm of nature for his survival; if he seeks to plunder nature indiscriminately that will perpetrate his own destruction. Indeed "like a seer Rabindranath had apprehended a crisis of this civilization through his extraordinary foresight and had imagined a way of survival" (Mitra 36; my translation).

(b) *Diggers' dance*

The Headman reports to Governor how Ranjan had instilled joy even in the diggers at their drudgery: "He cheered them up, and asked them to have a diggers' dance...". The absence of drums was compensated by beating the spades. As the Headman thundered Ranjan said, "I have unbound the work.... It won't have to be dragged out by force any more, it will run along of itself, dancing" (30). Tagore held that when man works in joy, work can give him a kind of freedom. In this machine-ruled civilization work means compulsion and drudgery, it carries no release, no joy. The diggers' dance offers a tentative solution to the crisis of today when the worker is alienated from his work and reduced to compulsive drudgery. But the rulers of Yaksha Town are not only impercipient to the idea, they are scared of it as well. So they issue the opinion, 'the fellow is mad'.

(v) The Stage

(a) A written script and the play-on-stage are certainly not the same thing. Shambhu Mitra, the eminent script-writer and actor, who is also known for his famous stage-production of *Raktakarabī*, explained how on-stage performance brings out a living manifestation of dynamic reality simultaneously at multiple layers. And when a novelist or a story-writer turns to play-writing, even a writer like Rabindranath with his peerless command of expression, the author looks for this assistance from the performance of the play.

(b) Rabindranath did not leave many detailed instructions in parenthetic notes like many a dramatist before and after him. He preferred to leave it to the creative imagination of sympathetic actors and directors.

(c) Tagore was against the use of drop-scene; he held that in order to indicate the change of act or scene, it could be sufficient if you just switched off the light once, and then switched it on again.

(d) Tagore was against crude imitation of reality in the stage-setting on the ground that an excessive adherence to realistic detail proved a hindrance to the free play of imagination in the spectator's mind; furthermore a fixed backdrop/screen at the back of the stage did not tally with the dynamism of the action. He thought this concern with creating optical illusion amounted to a kind of injustice to literature and a device suitable only for children's distraction. He also claimed that this was not the practice in ancient India or Greece where the actors and the spectators focused their attention upon the literary and dramatic core/content of the play.

Tagore wrote in the Preface to his play *Tapatī*:

> In the stage-planning of modern European drama the scene[backdrop] has entered as a kind of disturbance. This is childishness. This is the effort to dazzle the vision. This is a gate-crasher in the realm of literature and dramaturgy.... The idea of the tapovan in Sakuntala is given in the poetry itself. That is sufficient. That it has not been over-specified through a painting is

> itself congenial for the spectator's mind which can move freely. The drama makes its demands upon the spectator's imagination; the painting would have belittled it, and the loss would have been on the spectators' part. Acting is a dynamic, vibrant thing; the backdrop is its opposite. After making its unrightful entry into the dynamism it remains dumb, dull, and inert. By putting up a fixed fence before the spectator's view it keeps the vision constrained within limits. Where the mind should have taken its own space, a picture is imposed to bid farewell to the mind. This has been introduced in this era of mechanical devices; it was not so in the past. (my translation)

Tagore refers to the traditional folkforms of India, the *Yātrāpālā*, where no such delimiting scene constricts the vision and mind. In this context we can mention the return to folkform in Girish Karnad and Shambhu Mitra among major Indian dramatists of the post-Tagorean era. Tagore insisted about half a century before either Mitra or Karnad on the removal of so-called realistic appliances from the stage:

> It is for this very reason that wherever I have some control over the stage management I don't allow this childish practice of drawing up and dropping down the screen every now and then. This mocks the truth of reality and hinders the truth of imagination.

This applies to all his later plays.

(e) In *Red Oleanders*, in particular, only one scene provides the backdrop for the entire play. This is largely like *Yātrāpālā* or folk theatre, or Sanskrit theatre, in which all gather and disperse at the same open space. Everything goes on within the open space in front of the net of King, including even the supposedly confidential exchange between Governor and his men. The spectator knows and understands. Thus Tagore proves himself to be the foremost avant-garde theatrical practitioner of his time as he uses the age-old heritage of folkforms to articulate the most modern message/subject. Thus by saying

> little he can suggest a lot as he ensures the creative co-operation of the spectator in imaginatively conferring elasticity to the stage—telescoping or stretching distances between characters. The play validates Tagore's opinion that the theatre-stage does not require the realistic scene and backdrop of the movie.

It may be noted that the play was not staged during Tagore's lifetime.

(vi) Costume

While preparing for the stage presentation of *Raktakarabī* Shambhu Mitra had felt a bit intrigued about the appropriate costume of the King, because the old sign of thunder which used to be in currency in ancient India as the royal insignia might not be understood by the present-day audience. Then Nandalal Basu, the famous artist and ashramic of Shantiniketan, suggested the idea of using toothed wheel as a sign on the tunic, which he held to be an international item in today's world. The idea of a King is immediately associated in our mind with long sword, grand headgear, and other such gorgeous equipage. But Nandalal Basu instantly dismissed the idea, as he thought this 'King' represented modern man's scientific mind. Mitra's troupe 'Bahurupi' took special care in simultaneously disclosing and concealing the King towards the end when he would break through the net.

> In our theatre even when the King came out towards the end, no light was cast upon him. Only the gleam of a faint reflection of all the other lights cast on other people and items fell on the King. Only once a very faint light fell in a slant upon his back; it showed up distinctly the toothed wheel on his shirt back. The King's face was never seen; even his body too was seen only indistinctly as a shadow. (Mitra; my translation)

On the other hand the diggers, including Bishu, were given the dress of laborers; they were shown drinking liquor on-stage. Gosain must be unmistakable with his identity trade-mark of one who trades religion,—the white dhoti, scarf and sandalpaste-smeared forehead. Nandini's special costume is of course defined by the text itself, complete with her rice-coloured sari, and floral ornaments of red oleander; thus as soon as she appears on the stage she stands apart from the rest.

The Mythical Dimension

The spatial backdrop, the time-frame, the characters, anonymous as well as individualized, various allusions and touches in the script, including occasional fine details, relate to and stir up a range of mythic evocations/associations/signs—and all this together lend a mythical dimension to the play.

(i) In order to describe Ranjan, or 'youth' which floods over all barriers of rules with its dynamic force, the playwright uses the analogies of rowing across the turbulent river during cyclone, riding the wild horse through the forest by holding the mane, shooting the arrow at the exact midpoint between the eyebrows of the springing tiger, churning the strong current of the fast flowing hilly rivulet—these seem to be pictures restored from a hoary mythic world. Yet the author claims it to be a play about the modern times. Mitra wonders if these have been gleaned from Sanskrit literature, or from our old legends? These seem to have an affinity with our folklore. "The myths in currency in various parts of India in the folklores of various languages since ancient times—including the community tales of primitive tribes like the Kol, Bhil, Santhal—these images have been gleaned from the mines of that folk-memory to suggest an archetype of youth which refuses to surrender, which destroys to renew again and again." (Mitra 47-48; my translation)

(ii) Characters like Ranjan, Nandini, King, who are also archetypes, are presented side by side with distinct individuals like Phagulal-Chandra-Gokul. This can remind us of a very old tradition in our *Yātrāpālā*, in which 'Bibek' (conscience incarnate) used to move about on the stage perfectly at ease with royalties and villagers. Later figures representing 'Bharatmata', 'Niyati'(fate), etc., also appeared on our theatre stage and took part in the action even during the decade when *Raktakarabi* was written.

Thus the play seems to anticipate "a unique modern form of Indian dramatic tradition—a form in which the deepest and most complex thoughts of today can be projected by means of a distinct Indian idiom. It is not by imitating the structure of some Sanskrit play, or by adapting the frame of some folk theatre" (Mitra 48; trans. Present author).

Indeed Rabindranath here seems to show the way how to present in dramatic form, the crisis of civilization, the cruelty of the depersonalized system that have come up at the cost of personal relationships, and is bent on repressing life, on destroying youth,—in short the fascinating tale of the Yaksha Town at an apocalyptic time. He seems to reconcile the solid specificity of the stage with the impalpable but deeply stirring evocations from our racial memory, the collective memory of our folklore, and thus achieves a spectacular effect by means of stirring deep chords within us.

(iii) Some of the characters are simultaneously real human beings at one level, and symbols at another—not realistic but true. For instance, one can cite Nandini's description of King to Bishu:

> Like a man from the epics,—his forehead like the gateway of a tower, his arms the iron bolts of some inaccessible fortress.... A falcon was sitting on his left wrist. (22)

Again,

> It was as if he were a thousand-year-old banyan tree, and I a tiny little bird.... (23)

Rabindranath seems to move at ease between these different layers of realism and myth, and thus touches deep layers within our mind in flashes. The mythic evocation ushers in crowded emotions and associations which enrich our response.

(iv) Some other details also suggest the telescoping of times which is natural in the magic realism of myths; for instance, although it is a city of machines, Governor's wife rides a car drawn by bullocks, and when bullocks are unavailable the diggers are pressed into service. One is reminded of Kafka's surreal castle-village in his novel *The Castle*, where there is telephone link as well as man-driven sledge.

(v) Professor explains to Nandini, "The *Jinn* of that dead wealth we invoke. If we can enslave him the whole world lies at our feet" (4); this seems to evoke the legendary past of the *1001 Arabian Nights.*

(vi) Again, he says, the Yaksha Town is under eclipse; "The Shadow Demon, who lives in the gold caves, has eaten into it" (6). Here is a conflation of the ancient Hindu myths about the empirical phenomenon of eclipse and the fractured swallowing ways of the dark town; whereas eclipse takes place on the open space of the sky, here paradoxically it is an underground process carried on in darkness. Eclipse itself was considered inauspicious and ominous by the ancient people. Hence the effectiveness of the evocation.

(vii) The labyrinth that takes one further and further inwards—"as soon as one enters the maw of Yaksha Town, its jaws shut fast, and the one road that remains open leads withinwards" (14)—seems to carry the echo of so many legends and folklores across the world, registering the terror and confusion embedded in the racial memory regarding some mysterious power. One can also recall the Argentine writer J.L. Borges's magic realistic evocation of a 'labyrinth' as an archetypal symbol of frustrating bafflement and enigma in his story 'The Immortals', written nearly half-a-century after *Red Oleanders.*

> I have said that the city was founded on a stone plateau. ...in the rear was a pit, in the pit a stairway which sank down abysmally into the darkness below. I went down; through a chaos of

sordid galleries I reached a vast circular chamber, scarcely visible. There were nine doors in this cellar; eight led to a labyrinth that treacherously returned to the same chamber (through another labyrinth). (Borges, J.L. 139)

(viii) The song that permeates the action is also part of age-old harvesting rituals—one of those rituals which generated the great myths of mankind. In this connection, it may be pointed out that certain ritual aspects of theatre have been increasingly appearing in the avant-garde drama in India, particularly since the '70s, which Victor Turner would have called 'performing ethnography' (63). In his essay "Are there Universals of Performance in Myth, Ritual and Drama?" Turner, who had first hand experience of Indian drama, discusses the "developmental relationship from ritual to theatre" and maintains that "both ritual and theatre crucially involve liminal events and processes and have an important aspect of social metacommentary" (Turner 63). In this context Turner also rightly points out that theatre is the inheritor of that great multifaceted system of preindustrial ritual which embraces ideas and images of cosmos and chaos, interdigitates clowns and their foolery with gods and their solemnity, and uses all the sensory codes to produce symphonies in more than music: the intertwining of dance, body languages of many kinds, song, chant, architectural forms, incense, offerings, ritualized feasting and drinking, body painting, as also the enacting of mythic and heroic plots drawn from oral traditions (Turner 65). Tagore can be considered a trend-setter for modern Indian drama in this regard.

(ix) Bishu's narrating of the lure of golden spires—seems to resonate with the collective memory of so many folklores.

(x) The feather of the blue bird (28) floats in from the treasure of European myths from which Materlink took his 'blue bird'; again the blue-throated bird is also to be found in the dream-studded folklore of rural Bengal, which has been poignantly used by contemporary Bengali novelist Atin Bandyopadhya in his epic novel of partition,—*Nīlkaṇtha Pākhīr Sandhāne* (In search of the blue-throated bird).

(xi) Worship of the Flag and Weapons (11) also carries trace from ancient myths and rituals, once common and perhaps not entirely obsolete even today, though Tagore applies in the specific context of the play only.

Nandini. "Your God of the Flagstaff—he will never unbend". (44)

Finally, the King breaks the flagstaff while inviting Nandini 'to tear its banner' (48). Thus together they challenge and reject the myth installed by Yaksha Town.

The King, declaring war against his own prison emerges as the supreme mythical conclusion of a play resonating with so many mythical echoes.

(xii) The allusion to Lakshmi and Kuber in order to highlight the contrast between beautiful wealth and ugly accumulation can be traced back to an essay written just a few years before the play. In this essay written in 1328 Tagore made a differentiation between Lakshmi and Kuber, the deity of wealth and the deity of accumulation:

For seven months at a stretch I had been in America, the demonic citadel of wealth. There I have seen the face of consumerism, but not joy. I do not use the term demon (*dānab*) in any derogatory sense; had I been writing in English perhaps I would have said, titanic wealth, that is such wealth power is immense, whose volume is huge. Everyday I used to sit by the window in my hotel room under the frown of thirty/thirty-five floor buildings, and said to myself, Lakshmi is one and Kuber is another—a world of difference lies between them. The essential message of Lakshmi is benediction, by which wealth acquires beauty. The principle of Kuber is accumulation

> by which treasure multiplies. But sheer multiplication has no absolute meaning. Whosoever has been caught in this ceaseless race of acquiring more and more, becomes obsessed, dizzied, and rushes on inebriated with the addiction.... Sitting in the concrete jungle on the other side of the Atlantic my mind shrieked in pain, Where is the music amidst all this endless noise? I must have more and more and more—this message cannot acquire the melody of creation.
>
> ('Sikṣhar Milan'. *Kālāntar*; my translation)

Real and True

Tagore wrote in 1925 about *Red Oleanders*: "this book, which, being a mere translation, can have no pretension to a permanent place as literature in a language not the author's own". Yet Tagore had also claimed that this play was based on 'truth'. And truth, as we know, ensures its own perennial position and universal appeal. Is this the truth of facts, actuality, realism, or the truth of authentic perception inferred from the essence of human predicament? It is perhaps for the reader/audience to decide.

References

Barthes. *S/Z*. Trans. Richard Miller. N.Y.: Hill and Wang, 1974.

Bhattacharya, Upendranath. *Rabīndranātya Parikramā*. Kolkata: Orient Book Company, 1379 (Bengali Year).

Bishi, Pramathanath. *Rabīndranātyaprabāha* (1966). Kolkata: Orient Book Company, 1988.

Bloom, H. *The Anxiety of Influence* (1973). London: OUP Paperback, 1975.

Borges, J.L. "The Immortal", *Labyrinths*. (1964). N.Y.: Penguin Books, 1987.

Dasgupta, Shantikumar. *Rabīndranāther Rūpak Nātya*. Kolkata: Bharati Prakashani, 1392 (Bengali Year).

Foucault, M. *The Foucault Reader* (ed. Paul Rabinow). London: Penguin Books, 1991.

Mitra, Shambhu. *Nāṭak Raktakarabī*. Kolkata: M.C. Sarkar & Sons Pvt. Ltd., 1992. rpt. 2004.

Orwell, George. *Animal Farm* (1945). Orient Longman Limited (Indian Edition), 1995.

Sikdar, Ashrukumar. *Rabīndranāṭya: Rūpāntar O Oikya*. Kolkata: Grantha Nilay, 1374 (Bengali Year).

Tagore, Rabindranath. *The English Writings of Rabindranath Tagore*, (Vol. 3-Vol. 7). New Delhi: Atlantic Publishers & Distributors, 2007. [mentioned as *EWT*]

Turner, Victor. "Are there Universals of Performance in Myth, Ritual and Drama?". *Modern Theories of Drama* [Ed. G.W. Brandt]. Oxford: Clarendon Press, 1998.

Rama Kundu

Red Oleanders

A DRAMA IN ONE ACT

The curtain rises on a window covered by a network of intricate pattern in front of the Palace.

[Nandini and Kishôr, *a digger boy, come in.*]

Kishôr. Have you enough flowers, Nandini? Here, I have brought some more.

Nandini. Run away, Kishôr, do,—back to your work, quick! You'll be late again.

Kishôr. I must steal some time from my digging and digging of nuggets to bring out flowers to you.

Nandini. But they'll punish you, my boy, if they know.

Kishôr. You said you *must* have red oleanders. I am glad they're hard to find in this place. Only one tree I discovered after days of search, nearly hidden away behind a rubbish heap.

Nandini. Show it me. I'll go and gather the flowers myself.

Kishôr. Don't be cruel, Nandini. This tree is my one secret which none shall know. I've always envied Bishu, he can sing to you songs that are his own. From now I shall have flowers which you'll have to take only from my hands.

Nandini. But it breaks my heart to know that those brutes punish you.

Kishôr. It makes these flowers all the more preciously mine. They come from my pain.

Nandini. It pains me to accept anything which brings you hurt.

Kishôr. I dream of dying one day for your sake, Nandini.

Nandini. Is there nothing I can give you in return?

Kishôr. Promise that you will accept flowers only from me every morning.

Nandini. I will. But do be careful.

Kishôr. No, no, I shall be rash and defy their blows. My homage shall be my daily triumph. [*Goes.*]

[Professor *comes in.*]

Professor. Nandini!

Nandini. Yes, Professor!

Professor. Why do you come and startle one, now and again, and then pass by? Since you awaken a cry in our hearts, what harm if you stop a moment in answer to it? Let us talk a little.

Nandini. What need have you of me?

Professor. If you talk of need, look over there!—You'll see our tunnel-diggers creeping out of the holes like worms, with loads of things of need. In this Yaksha Town all our treasure is of gold, the secret treasure of the dust. But the gold which is you, beautiful one, is not of the dust, but of the light which never owns any bond.

Nandini. Over and over again you say this to me. What makes you wonder at me so, Professor?

Professor. The sunlight gleaming through the forest thickets surprises nobody, but the light that breaks through a cracked wall is quite a different thing. In Yaksha Town, you are this light that startles. Tell me, what d'you think of this place?

Nandini. It puzzles me to see a whole city thrusting its head underground, groping with both hands in the dark. You dig tunnels in the underworld and come out with dead wealth that the earth has kept buried for ages past.

Professor. The *Jinn* of that dead wealth we invoke. If we can enslave him the whole world lies at our feet.

Nandini. Then again, you hide your king behind a wall of netting. Is it for fear of people finding out that he's a man?

Professor. As the ghost of our dead wealth is fearfully potent so is our ghostly royalty, made hazy by this net, with its inhuman power to frighten people.

Nandini. All you say is a kind of made-up talk.

Professor. Of course made-up. The naked is without a credential, it's the made-up clothes that define us. It delights me immensely to discuss philosophy with you.

Nandini. That's strange! You who burrow day and night in a mass of yellow pages, like your diggers in the bowels of the earth,—why waste your time on me?

Professor. The privilege of wasting time proves one's wealth of time. We poor drudges are insects in a hole in this solid toil, you are the evening star in the rich sky of leisure. When we see you, our wings grow restless. Come to my room. For a moment allow me to be reckless in my waste of time.

Nandini. No, not now. I have come to see your king, in *his* room.

Professor. How can you enter through the screen?

Nandini. I shall find my way through the net-work.

Professor. Do you know, Nandini, I too live behind a net-work of scholarship. I am an unmitigated scholar, just as our king is an unmitigated king.

Nandini. You are laughing at me, Professor. But tell me, when they brought me here, why didn't they bring my Rañjan also?

Professor. It's their way to snatch things by fractions. But why should you want to drag your life's treasure down amongst this dead wealth of ours?

Nandini. Because I know he can put a beating heart behind these dead ribs.

Professor. Your own presence is puzzling enough for our governors here; if Rañjan also comes they will be in despair.

Nandini. They do not know how comic they are,—Rañjan will bring God's own laughter in their midst and startle them into life.

Professor. Divine laughter is the sunlight that melts ice, but not stones. Only the pressure of gross muscle can move our governors.

Nandini. My Rañjan's strength is like that of your river, Sankhini,—it can laugh and yet it can break. Let me tell you a little secret news of mine. I shall meet Rañjan to-day.

Professor. Who told you that?

Nandini. Yes, yes, we shall meet. The news has come.

Professor. Through what way could news come and yet evade the Governor?

Nandini. Through the same way that brings news of the coming Spring.

Professor. You mean it's in the air,—like the rumours which flush in the colour of the sky, or flutter in the dance of the wind?

Nandini. I won't say more now. When Rañjan comes you'll see for yourself how rumours in the air come down on earth.

Professor. Once she begins to talk of Rañjan there's no stopping Nandini's mouth! Well, well, I have my books, let me take my shelter behind them,—I dare not go on with this. [*Coming back after going a little way.*] Nandini. Let me ask you one thing. Aren't you frightened of our Yaksha Town?

Nandini. Why should I feel afraid?

Professor. All creatures fear an eclipse, not the full sun. Yaksha Town is a city under eclipse. The Shadow Demon, who lives in the gold caves, has eaten into it. It is not whole itself, neither does it allow any one else to remain whole. Listen to me, don't stay here. When you go, these pits will yawn all the wider for us, I know,—yet I say to you, fly; go and live happily with Rañjan where people in their drunken fury don't tear the earth's veil to pieces. [*Going a little way and then coming back.*] Nandini, will you give me a flower from your chain of red oleanders?

Nandini. Why, what will you do with it?

Professor. How often have I thought that there is some omen in these ornaments of yours.

Nandini. I don't know of any.

Professor. Perhaps your fate knows. In that red there is not only beauty, but also the fascination of fear.

Nandini. Fear! Even in me?

Professor. I don't know what event you have come to write with that crimson tint. There was the gardenia and the tuberose, there was white jasmine,—why did you leave them all and choose this flower? Do you know, we often choose our own fate thus, without knowing it!

Nandini. Rañjan sometimes calls me Red Oleander. I feel that the colour of his love is red,—that red I wear on my neck, on my breast, on my arms.

Professor. Well, just give me one of those flowers,—a moment's gift,—let me try to understand the meaning of its colour.

Nandini. Here, take it. Rañjan is coming to-day,—out of my heart's delight I give it to you. [Professor *goes.*]

[Gôkul, *a digger, comes in.*]

Gôkul. Turn this way, woman! Who are you? I've never yet been able to understand you.

Nandini. I'm nothing more than what you see. What need have you to understand me?

Gôkul. I don't trust what I can't understand. For what purpose has the King brought you here?

Nandini. Because I serve no purpose of his.

Gôkul. You know some spell, I'm sure. You're snaring everybody here. You're a witch! Those who are bewitched by your beauty will come to their death.

Nandini. That death will not be yours, Gôkul, never fear! You'll die digging.

Gôkul. Let me see, let me see, what's that dangling over your forehead?

Nandini. Only a tassel of red oleanders.

Gôkul. What does it mean?

Nandini. It has no meaning at all.

Gôkul. I don't believe you, one bit! You're up to some trickery. Some evil will befall us before the day is out. That's why you have got yourself up like this. Oh you terrible, terrible witch!

Nandini. What makes you think me so terrible?

Gôkul. You're looking like an ominous torch.

Nandini. The autumn song:

Hark, 'tis Autumn calling:
'Come, O, come away!'—
Her basket is heaped with corn.

Don't you see the September sun is spreading the glow of the ripening corn in the air?

Drunken with the perfumed wine of wind,
the sky seems to sway among the
shivering corn,
its sunlight trailing on the fields.

You too come out, King!—out into the fields.

Voice. Fields! What could I do there?

Nandini. The work there is much simpler than your work in Yaksha Town.

Voice. It's the simple which is impossible for me. A lake cannot run out dancing, like a frolicsome waterfall. Leave me now, I have no time.

Nandini. The day you let me into your store-house the blocks of gold did not surprise me,—what amazed me was the immense strength with which you lifted and arranged them. But can blocks of gold ever answer to the swinging rhythm of your arms in the same way as fields of corn? Are you not afraid, King, of handling the dead wealth of the earth?

Voice. What is there to fear?

Nandini. The living heart of the earth gives itself up in love and life and beauty, but when you rend its bosom and disturb the dead, you bring up with your booty the curse of its dark demon, blind and hard, cruel and envious. Don't you see everybody here is either angry, or suspicious, or afraid?

Voice. Curse?

Nandini. Yes, the curse of grabbing and killing.

Voice. But we bring up strength. Does not my strength please you, Nandini?

Nandini. Indeed it does. Therefore I ask you, come out into the light, step on the ground, let the earth be glad.

Voice. Do you know, Nandini, you too are half-hidden behind an evasion,—you mystery of beauty! I want to pluck you out of it, to grasp you within my closed fist, to handle you, scrutinise you,—or else to break you to pieces.

Nandini. Whatever do you mean?

Voice. Why can't I strain out the tint of your oleanders and build a dream out of it to keep before my eyes? Those few frail petals guard it and hinder me. Within you there is the same hindrance, so strong because so soft. Nandini, will you tell me what you think of me?

Nandini. Not now, you have no time. Let me go.

Voice. No, no, don't go. Do tell me what you think of me.

Nandini. Have I not told you often enough? I think you are wonderful. Strength swelling up in your arms, like rolling clouds before a storm,—it makes my heart dance within me.

Voice. And when your heart dances to see Rañjan, is that also—

Nandini. Let that be,—you have no time.

Voice. There is time,—for this; only tell me, then go.

Nandini. That dance rhythm is different, you won't understand.

Voice. I will, I must understand.

Nandini. I can't explain it clearly. Let me go.

Voice. Tell me, at least, whether you like me.

Nandini. Yes, I like you.

Voice. The same as Rañjan?

Nandini. Again the same question! I tell you, you don't understand these things.

Voice. I *do* understand, a little. I know what the difference is between Rañjan and me. In me there is only strength, in Rañjan there is magic.

Nandini. What d'you mean by magic?

Voice. Shall I explain? Underground there are blocks of stone, iron, gold,—there you have the image of strength. On the surface grows the grass, the flower blossoms,—there you have the play of magic. I can extract gold from the fearsome depths of secrecy, but to wrest that magic from the near at hand I fail.

Nandini. You have no end of things, yet why always covet?

Voice. All I possess is so much dead weight. No increase of gold can create a particle of a touchstone, no increase of power can ever come up to youth. I can only guard by force. If I had Rañjan's youth I could leave you free and yet hold you fast. My time is spent in knotting the binding rope, but, alas, everything else can be kept tied, except joy.

Nandini. It is you who entangle yourself in your own net, then why keep on fretting?

Voice. You will never understand. I, who am a desert, stretch out my hand to you, a tiny blade of grass, and cry: I am parched, I am bare, I am weary. The flaming thirst of this desert licks up one fertile field after another, only to enlarge itself,—it can never annex the life of the frailest of grasses.

Nandini. One would never think you were so tired.

Voice. One day, Nandini, in a far off land, I saw a mountain as weary as myself. I could not guess that all its stones were aching inwardly. One night I heard a noise, as if some giant's evil dream had moaned and moaned and suddenly snapped asunder. Next morning I found the mountain had disappeared in the chasm of a yawning earthquake. That made me understand how overgrown power crushes itself inwardly by its own weight. I see in you something quite opposite.

Nandini. What is it you see in me?

Voice. The dance rhythm of the All.

Nandini. I don't understand.

Voice. The rhythm that lightens the enormous weight of matter. To that rhythm the bands of stars and planets go about dancing from sky to sky, like so many minstrel boys. It is that rhythm, Nandini, that makes you so simple, so perfect. How small you are compared to me, yet I envy you.

Nandini. You have cut yourself off from everybody and so deprived yourself.

Voice. I keep myself apart, that it may become easy for me to plunder the world's big treasure-houses. Nevertheless there are gifts that your little flower-like fingers can easily reach, but not all the strength of my body,—gifts hidden in God's closed hand. That hand I must force open some day.

Nandini. When you talk like that, I don't follow you. Let me go.

Voice. Go then; but here, I stretch out this hand of mine from my window, place your hand on it for a moment.

Nandini. Only a hand, and the rest of you hidden? It frightens me!

Voice. Everybody flies from me because they only see my hand. But if I wished to hold you with all of me, would you come to me, Nandini?

Nandini. Why talk like this when you wouldn't even let me come into your room?

Voice. My busy time, overloaded with work, dragged along against obstruction, is not for you. On the day when you can arrive, full sail before the wind, into the bosom of my full.

Phágulal. Isn't it our holiday? Yesterday was the feast day of the War Goddess. To-day they worship the Flag.

Chandrá. Must you drink just because it's a holiday? In our village home, on feast days, you never—

Phágulal. Freedom itself was enough for the holidays in our village. The caged bird spends its holiday knocking against the bars. In Yaksha Town holidays are more of a nuisance than work.

Chandrá. Let's go back home, then.

Phágulal. The road to our home is closed for ever.

Chandrá. How's that?

Phágulal. Our homes don't yield them any profit.

Chandrá. But are we closely fitted to their profits only,—like husks to grains of corn,—with nothing of us left over?

Phágulal. Our mad Bishu says: to remain whole is useful only for the lamb itself; those who eat it prefer to leave out its horns and hooves, and even object to its bleating when butchered.

[*There's the madcap, singing as he goes.*]

Chandrá. It's only the last few days that his songs have burst forth.

Phágulal. That's true.

Chandrá. He's been possessed by Nandini. She draws his heart and his songs too.

Phágulal. No wonder.

Chandrá. Indeed! You'd better be careful. She'll next be bringing out songs from *your* throat,—which would be rough on our neighbours. The witch is up to all kinds of tricks, and is sure to bring misfortune.

Phágulal. Bishu's misfortune is nothing recent, he knew Nandini long before coming here.

Chandrá [*calling out*]. I say, Bishu, come this way. Maybe you'll find somebody here also to listen to your singing,—it won't be altogether thrown away.

[Bishu *comes in, singing.*]

Bishu [*sings*].

Boatman of my dreams,
The sail is filled with a boisterous breeze
and my mad heart sings
to the lilt of the rocking of thy boat,
at the call of the far away landing.

Chandrá. I know who the boatman of your dreams is.

Bishu. How should you know from outside? You haven't seen from inside my boat.

Chandrá. Your boat is going to get wrecked one of these days, let me tell you,—by that pet Nandini of yours.

[Gôkul, *the digger, comes in.*]

Gôkul. I say, Bishu, I don't quite trust your Nandini.

Bishu. Why, what has she done?

Gôkul. She does nothing, that's the rub. I don't understand the way she goes on.

Chandrá. To see her flaunting her prettiness all over the place makes me sick.

Gôkul. We can trust features that are plain enough to understand.

Bishu. I know the atmosphere of this place breeds contempt for beauty. There must be beauty even in hell; but nobody there can understand it, that's their cruellest punishment.

Chandrá. Maybe we are fools, but even our Governor here can't stand her—d'you know that?

Bishu. Take care, Chandrá, lest you catch the infection of our Governor's eyes—then perhaps yours too will redden at the sight of us. What say you, Phágulal?

Phágulal. To tell you the truth, brother, when I see Nandini, I feel ashamed to think of myself. I can't utter a word when she's there.

Gôkul. The day will come when you'll know her to your cost,—perhaps too late. [*Goes.*]

Phágulal. Bishu, your friend Chandrá wants to know why we drink.

Bishu. God in his mercy has everywhere provided a liberal allowance of drink. We men with our arms supply the output of our muscles, you women with yours supply the wine of embraces. In this world there is hunger to force us to work; but there's also the green of the woods, the gold of the sunshine, to make us drunk with their holiday-call.

Chandrá. You call these things *drink?*

Bishu. Yes, drinks of life, an endless stream of intoxication. Take my case. I come to this place; I am set to work burgling the underworld; for me nature's own ration of spirits is stopped; so my inner man craves the artificial wine of the market place. [*Sings.*]

My life, your sap has run dry,
Fill then the cup with the wine of death,
That flushes all emptiness with its laughter.

Chandrá. Come, brother, let us fly from here.

Bishu. To that boundless tavern, underneath the blue canopy? Alas, the road is closed, and we seek consolation in the stolen wine of the prison house. No open sky, no leisure for us; so we have distilled the essence of all the song and laughter, all the sunlight of the twelve hours' day into one draught of liquid fire. [*Sings.*]

Thy sun is hidden amid a mass of murky cloud.
Thy day has smudged itself black in dusty toil.
Then let the dark night descend
the last comrade of drunken oblivion,
Let it cover thy tired eyes with the mist
that will help thee desperately to lose thyself.

Chandrá. Well, well, Bishu, you men have gone to the dogs in Yaksha Town, if you like, but we women haven't changed at all.

Bishu. Haven't you? Your flowers have faded, and you are all slavering for gold.

Chandrá. No, never!

Bishu. I say, yes. That Phágulal toils for hours over and above the twelve,—why? For a reason unknown to him, unknown even to you. But I know. It's your dream of gold that lashes him on to work, more severely than the foreman's whip.

Chandrá. Very well. Then why don't we fly from here, and go back home?

Bishu. Your Governor has closed the way as well as the will to return. If you go there to-day you will fly back here to-morrow, like a caged bird to its cage, hankering for its drugged food.

Phágulal. I say, Bishu, once upon a time you came very near spoiling your eyesight poring over books; how is it they made you ply the spade along with the rest of us stupid boors?

Chandrá. All this time we've been here, we haven't got from Bishu the answer to this particular question.

Phágulal. Yet we all know it.

Bishu. Well, out with it then!

Phágulal. They employed you to spy on us.

Bishu. If you knew that, how is it you let me off alive?

Phágulal. But, we knew also, that game was not in your line.

Chandrá. How is it you couldn't stick to such a comfortable job, brother?

Bishu. Comfortable job? To stick to a living being like a carbuncle on his back?

I said: 'I must go home, my health is failing.'

'Poor thing,' said the Governor, 'how can you go home in such a state? However, there's no harm in your trying.'

Well, I did try. And then I found that, as soon as one enters the maw of Yaksha Town, its jaws shut fast, and the one road that remains open leads withinwards. Now I am swamped in that interior without hope and without light, and the only difference between you and me is, that the Governor looks down upon me even worse than upon you. Man despises the broken pot of his own creation more than the withered leaf fallen from the tree.

Phágulal. What does that matter, Bishu? You have risen high in our esteem.

Bishu. Discovery only means death. Where you favour falls there falls the Governor's glance. The more noisily the yellow frogs welcome the black toad, the sooner their croaking points him out to the boa-constrictor.

Chandrá. But when will your work be finished?

Bishu. The calendar never records the last day. After the first day comes the second, after the second the third. There's no such thing as getting finished here. We're always digging—one yard, two yards, three yards. We go on raising gold nuggets,—after one nugget another, then more and more and more. In Yaksha Town figures follow one another in rows and never arrive at any conclusion. That's why we are not men to them, but only numbers.—Phágu, what's yours?

Phágulal. I'm No. 47 V.

Bishu. I'm 69 Ng.

Chandrá. Brother, they've hoarded such heaps of gold, can't they stop digging now?

Bishu. There's always an end to things of need, no doubt; so we stop when we've had enough to eat. But we don't need drunkenness, therefore there's no end to it. These nuggets are the drink—the solid drink—of our Gold King. Don't you see?

Chandrá. No, I don't.

Bishu. Cups in hand, we forget that we are chained to our limits. Gold blocks in hand, our master fancies he's freed from the gravitation of the commonplace, and is soaring in the rarest of upper heights.

Chandrá. In this season the villages are preparing for their harvest festival. Let's go home.

Phágulal. Don't worry me, Chandrá. A thousand times over have I told you that in these parts there are high roads to the market, to the burning ground, to the scaffold,—everywhere except to the homeland.

Chandrá. If we were to go to the Governor, and just tell him—

Bishu. Hasn't your woman's wit seen through the Governor yet?

Chandrá. Why, he seems to be so nice and—

Bishu. Yes, nice and polished, like the crocodile's teeth, which fit into one another with so thorough a bite that the King himself can't unlock the jaw, even if he wants to.

Chandrá. There comes the Governor.

Bishu. Then it's all up with us. He's sure to have overheard—

Chandrá. Why, we haven't said anything so very—

Bishu. Sister, we can only say the words,—they put in the meaning.

[*The* Governor *comes in.*]

Chandrá. Sir Governor!

Governor. Well, my child?

Chandrá. Grant us leave to go home for a little.

Governor. Why, aren't the rooms we have given you excellent, much better than the ones at home? We have even kept a state watchman for your safety.

Hullo, 69 Ng, to see you amongst these people reminds one of a heron come to teach paddy birds how to cut capers.

Bishu. Sir, your jesting does not reassure me. Had my feet the strength to make others dance, would I not have run away from here, first thing? Especially after the striking examples I've seen of the fate that overtakes dancing masters in this country. As things are, one's legs tremble even to walk straight.

Chandrá. Give us leave, Sir Governor, do give us leave. Let us go just for once, and see our waving fields of barleycorn in the ear, and the ample shade of our banian tree with its hanging roots. I cannot tell you how our hearts ache. Don't you see that your men here work all day in the dark, and in the evening steep themselves in the denser dark of drunkenness? Have you no pity for them?

Governor. My dear child, surely you know of our constant anxiety for their welfare. That is exactly why I have sent for our High Preacher, Kenarám Gosain himself, to give moral talks to the men. Their votive fees will pay for his upkeep. Every evening the Gosain will come and—

Phágulal. That won't do, sir! Now, at worst, we get drunk of an evening, but if we are preached to every night, there'll be manslaughter!

Bishu. Hush, hush, Phágulal.

[*Preacher* Gosain *comes in.*]

Governor. Talk of the Preacher and he appears. Your Holiness, I do you reverence. These workmen of ours sometimes feel disturbed in their weak minds. Deign to whisper in their ears some texts of peace. The need is urgent.

Gosain. These people? Are they not the very incarnation of the sacred Tortoise of our scripture, that held up the sinking earth on its back? Because they meekly suppress themselves underneath their burden, the upper world can keep its head aloft. The very thought sends a thrill through my body!

Just think of it, friend 47 V, yours is the duty of supplying food to this mouth which chants the holy name. With the sweat of your brow have you woven this wrap printed with the holy name, which exalts this devoted body. Surely that is no mean privilege. May you remain for ever undisturbed, is my benediction, for then the grace of God will abide with you likewise.

My friends, repeat aloud the holy name of Hari, and all your burdens will be lightened. The name of Hari shall be taken in the beginning, in the middle, and at the end,—so say the scriptures.

Chandrá. How sweet! It's long since I have heard such words! Give, oh give me a little dust off your feet!

Phágulal. Stop this waste of money, Governor. If it's our offerings you want, we can stand it, but we're fairly sick of this cant.

Bishu. Once Phágulal runs amok it's all over with the lot of you. Hush, hush, Phágulal!

Chandrá. Are you bent on spoiling your chances both in this world and the next, you wretched man? You were never like this before. Nandini's ill wind has blown upon you,—and no mistake.

Gosain. What charming naiveté, Sir Governor! What's in their heart is always on their lips. What can we teach them?—it's they who'll teach us a lesson. You know what I mean.

Governor. I know where the root of the trouble is. I'll have to take them in hand myself, I see. Meanwhile, pray go to the next parish and chant them the holy name,—the sawyers there have taken to grumbling, somewhat.

Gosain. Which parish did you say?

Governor. Parish T-D. No. 71 T is headman there. It ends to the left of where No. 65 of Row M lives.

Gosain. My son, though Parish T-D may not yet be quieted, the whole Row of M's have lately become steeped in a beautiful spirit of meekness. Still it is better to keep an extra police force posted in the parish some time longer. Because, as you know our scripture says,—pride is our greatest foe. After the strength of the police has helped to conquer pride, then comes our turn. I take my leave.

Chandrá. Forgive these men, Your Holiness, and give them your blessing, that they may follow the right path.

Gosain. Fear not, good woman, they'll all end thoroughly pacified. [*The* Gosain *goes.*]

Governor. I say, 69 Ng, the temper of your parish seems to be somewhat strained.

Bishu. That's nothing strange. The Gosain called them the incarnation of the Tortoise. But, according to scripture, incarnations change; and, when the Tortoise gave place to the Boar, in place of hard shell came out aggressive teeth, so that all-suffering patience was transformed into defiant obstinacy.

Chandrá. But, Sir Governor, don't forget my request.

Governor. I have heard it and will bear it in mind. [*He goes.*]

Chandrá. Ah now, didn't you see how nice the Governor is? How he smiles every time he talks!

Bishu. Crocodile's teeth begin by smiling and end by biting.

Chandrá. Where does his bite come in?

Bishu. Don't you know he's going to make it a rule not to let the workmen's wives accompany them here.

Chandrá. Why?

Bishu. We have a place in their account book as numbers, but women's figures do not mate with figures of arithmetic.

Chandrá. O dear! but have they no women-folk of their own?

Bishu. Their ladies are besotted with the wine of gold, even worse than their husbands.

Chandrá. Bishu, you had a wife at home,—what's become of her?

Bishu. So long as I filled the honoured post of spy, they used to invite her to those big mansions to play cards with their ladies. Ever since I joined Phágulal's set, all that was stopped, and she left me in a huff at the humiliation.

Chandrá. For shame! But look, brother Bishu, what a grand procession! One palanquin after another! Don't you see the sparkle of the jewelled fringes of the elephant-seats? How beautiful the out-riders on horseback look, as if they had bits of sunlight pinned on the points of their spears!

Bishu. Those are the Governor's and Deputy Governor's ladies, going to the Flag-worship.

Chandrá. Bless my soul, what a gorgeous array and how fine they look!

I say, Bishu, if you hadn't given up that job, would you have gone along with that set in this grand style?—and that wife of yours surely—

Bishu. Yes, we too should have come to just such a pass.

Chandrá. Is there no way going back,—none whatever?

Bishu. There is,—through the gutter.

A Distant Voice. Bishu, my mad one!

Bishu. Yes, my mad girl!

Phágulal. There's Nandini. There'll be no more of Bishu for us, for the rest of the day.

Chandrá. Tell me, Bishu, what does she charm you with?

Bishu. The charm of sorrow.

Chandrá. Why do you talk so topsy-turvy?

Bishu. She reminds me that there are sorrows, to forget which is the greatest of sorrow.

Phágulal. Please to speak plainly, Bishu, otherwise it becomes positively annoying!

Bishu. The pain of desire for the near belongs to the animal, the sorrow of aspiration for the far belongs to man. That far away flame of my eternal sorrow is revealed through Nandini.

Chandrá. Brother, we don't understand these things. But one thing I do understand and that is,—the less you men can make out a girl, the more she attracts you! We simple women,—our price is not so high, but we at least keep you on the straight path. I warn you, once for all, that girl with her noose of red oleanders will drag you to perdition.

[Chandrá *and* Phágulal *go.*]

[Nandini *comes in.*]

Nandini. My mad one, did you hear their autumn songs this morning?

Bishu. Is my morning like yours that I should hear singing? Mine is only a swept-away remnant of the weary night.

Nandini. In my gladness of heart I thought I'd stand on the rampart and join in their song. But the guards would not let me, so I've come to you.

Bishu. I am not a rampart.

Nandini. You are *my* rampart. When I come to you I seem to climb high, I find the open light.

Bishu. Ever since coming to Yaksha Town the sky has dropped out of my life. I felt as if they had pounded me in the same mortar with all the fractions of men here, and rolled us into a solid lump.

Then you came and looked into my face in a way that made me sure some light could still be seen through me.

Nandini. In this closed fort a bit of sky survives only between you and me, my mad one.

Bishu. Through that sky my songs can fly towards you.

[*Sings.*]

You keep me awake that I may sing to you,
O Breaker of my sleep!
And so my heart you startle with your call,
O Waker of my grief!
The shades of evening fall,
the birds come to their nest.
The boat arrives ashore,
yet my heart knows no rest,
O Waker of my grief!

Nandini. The waker of your grief, Bishu?

Bishu. Yes, you are my messenger from the unreachable shore. The day you came to Yaksha Town a gust of salt air knocked at my heart.

Nandini. But I never had any message of this sorrow of which you sing.

Bishu. Not even from Rañjan?

Nandini. No, he holds an oar in each hand and ferries me across the stormy waters; he catches wild horses by the mane and rides with me through the woods; he shoots an arrow between the eyebrows of the tiger on the spring, and scatters my fear with loud laughter. As he jumps into our Nagai river and disturbs its current with his joyous splashing, so he disturbs me with his tumultuous life. Desperately he stakes his all on the game and thus has he won me.

You also were there with us, but you held aloof, and at last something urged you one day to leave our gambling set. At the time of your parting you looked at my face in a way I could not quite make out. After that I've had no news of you for long. Tell me where you went off to then.

Bishu. My boat was tied to the bank; the rope snapped; the wild wind drove it into the tackles unknown.

Nandini. But who dragged you back from there to dig for nuggets here in Yaksha Town?

Bishu. A woman. Just as a bird on the wing is brought to the ground by a chance arrow, so did she bring me down to the dust. I forgot myself.

Nandini. How could she touch you?

Bishu. When the thirsty heart despairs of finding water it's easy enough for it to be deluded by a mirage, and driven in barren quest from desert to desert.

One day, while I was gazing at the sunset clouds, she had her eye upon the golden spire of the Governor's palace. Her glance challenged me to take her over there. In my foolish pride I vowed to do so. When I did bring her here, under the golden spire, the spell was broken.

Nandini. I've come to take you away from here.

Bishu. Since you have moved even the king of this place, what power on earth can prevent you? Tell me, don't you feel afraid of him?

Nandini. I did fear him from outside that screen. But now I've seen him inside.

Bishu. What was he like?

Nandini. Like a man from the epics,—his forehead like the gateway of a tower, his arms the iron bolts of some inaccessible fortress.

Bishu. What did you see when you went inside?

Nandini. A falcon was sitting on his left wrist. He put it on the perch and gazed at my face. Then, just as he had been stroking the falcon's wings, he began gently to stroke my hand. After a while he suddenly asked: 'Don't you fear me, Nandini?'

'Not in the least,' said I.

Then he buried his fingers in my unbound hair and sat long with closed eyes.

Bishu. How did you like it?

Nandini. I liked it. Shall I tell you how? It was as if he were a thousand-year-old banyan tree, and I a tiny little bird; when I lit on a branch of his and had my little swing, he needs must have felt a thrill of delight to his very marrow. I loved to give that bit of joy to that lonely soul.

Bishu. Then what did he say?

Nandini. Starting up and fixing his spear-point gaze on my face, he suddenly said: 'I want to know you.'

I felt a shiver run down my body and asked: 'What is there to know?—I am not a manuscript!'

'I know all there is in manuscripts,' said he, 'but I don't know you.' Then he became excited and cried: 'Tell me all about Rañjan. Tell me how you love him.'

I talked on: 'I love Rañjan as the rudder in the water might love the sail in the sky, answering its rhythm of wind in the rhythm of waves.'

He listened quietly, staring like a big greedy boy. All of a sudden he startled me by exclaiming: 'Could you die for him?'

'This very moment,' I replied.

'Never,' he almost roared, as if in anger.

'Yes, I could,' I repeated.

'What good would that do you?'

'I don't know,' said I.

Then he writhed and shouted: 'Go away from my room, go, go at once, don't disturb me in my work.'

I could not understand what that meant.

Bishu. He gets angry when he can't understand.

Nandini. Bishu, don't you feel pity for him?

Bishu. The day when God will be moved to pity for him, he will die.

Nandini. No, no, you don't know how desperately he wants to live.

Bishu. You will see this very day what his living means. I don't know whether you'll be able to bear the sight.

Nandini. There, look, there's a shadow. I am sure the Governor has secretly heard what we've been saying.

Bishu. This place is dark with the Governor's shadow, it is everywhere. How do you like him?

Nandini. I have never seen anything so lifeless,—like a cane stick cut from the cane bush,—no leaves, no roots, no sap in the veins.

Bishu. Cut off from life, he spends himself in repressing life.

Nandini. Hush, he will hear you.

Bishu. He hears even when you are silent, which is all the more dangerous. When I am with the diggers I am careful in my speech, so much so that the Governor thinks I'm the sorriest of the lot, and spares me out of sheer contempt. But, my mad girl, when I am with you my mind scorns to be cautious.

Nandini. No, no, you must not court danger. There comes the Governor.

[*The* Governor *comes in.*]

Governor. Hallo, 69 Ng! you seem to be making friends with everybody, without distinction.

Bishu. You may remember that I began by making friends even with you, only it was the distinction that stood in the way.

Governor. Well, what are we discussing now?

Bishu. We are discussing how to escape from this fortress of yours.

Governor. Really? So recklessly, that you don't even mind confessing it?

Bishu. Sir Governor, it doesn't need much cleverness to know that when a captive bird pecks at the bars it's not in the spirit of caress. What does it matter whether that's openly confessed or not?

Governor. The captives' want of love we were aware of, but their not fearing to admit it has become evident only recently.

Nandini. Won't you let Rañjan come?

Governor. You will see him this very day.

Nandini. I knew that; still, for your message of hope I wish you victory. Governor, take this garland of *kunda* flowers.

Governor. Why throw away the garland thus, and not keep it for Rañjan?

Nandini. There is a garland for him.

Governor. Aha, I thought so! I suppose it's the one hanging round your neck. The garland of victory may be of *kunda* flowers, the gift of the hand; but the garland of welcome is of red oleanders, the gift of the heart. Well, let's be quick in accepting what comes from the hand, for that will fade; as for the heart's offering, the longer it waits the more precious it grows. [*The* Governor *goes.*]

Nandini [*knocking at the window*]. Do you hear? Let me come into your room.

Voice [*from behind the scenes*]. Why always the same futile request? Who is that with you? A pair to Rañjan?

Bishu. No, King, I am the obverse side of Rañjan, on which falls the shadow.

Voice. What use has Nandini for you?

Bishu. The use which music has for the hollow of the flute.

Voice. Nandini, what is this man to you?

Nandini. He's my partner in music. My heart soars in his voice, my pain cries in his tunes,—that's what he tells me. [*Sings*.]

'I love, I love,'— 'Tis the cry that breaks out
from the bosom of earth and water.

Voice. So that's your partner! What if I dissolved your partnership this very minute?

Nandini. Why are you so cross? Haven't you any companion yourself?

Voice. Has the mid-day sun any companion?

Nandini. Well, let's change the subject. What's that? What's that in your hand?

Voice. A dead frog.

Nandini. What for?

Voice. Once upon a time this frog got into a hole in a stone, and in that shelter it existed for three thousand years. I have learnt from it the secret of continuing to exist, but to live it does not know. To-day I felt bored and smashed its shelter. I've thus saved it from existing for ever. Isn't that good news?

Nandini. Your stone walls will also fall away from around me to-day,—I shall meet Rañjan.

Voice. I want to see you both together.

Nandini. You won't be able to see from behind your net.

Voice. I shall let you sit inside my room.

Nandini. What will you do with us?

Voice. Nothing, I only want to know you.

Nandini. When you talk of knowing, it frightens me.

Voice. Why?

Nandini. I feel that you have no patience with things that cannot be known, but can only be felt.

Voice. I dare not trust such things lest they should play me false. Now go away, don't waste my time.—No, no, wait a little. Give me that tassel of red oleanders which hangs from your hair.

Nandini. What will you do with it?

Voice. When I look at those flowers it seems to me as if the red light of my evil star has appeared in their shape. At times I want to snatch them from you and tear them to pieces. Again I think that if Nandini were ever to place that spray of flowers on my head, with her own hands, then—

Nandini. Then what?

Voice. Then perhaps I might die in peace.

Nandini. Some one loves red oleanders and calls me by that name. It is in remembrance of him that I wear these flowers.

Voice. Then, I tell you, they're going to be *his* evil star as well as *mine.*

Nandini. Don't say such things for shame! I am going.

Voice. Where?

Nandini. I shall go and sit near the gate of your fort.

Voice. Why?

Nandini. When Rañjan comes he'll see I am waiting for him.

Voice. I should like to tread hard on Rañjan and grind him in the dust.

Nandini. Why pretend to frighten me?

Voice. Pretend, you say? Don't you know I am really fearsome?

Nandini. You seem to take pleasure in seeing people frightened at you. In our village plays Srikantha takes the part of a demon; when he comes on the stage, he is delighted if the children are terrified. You are like him. Do you know what I think?

Voice. What is it?

Nandini. The people here trade on frightening others. That's why they have put you behind a network and dressed you fantastically. Don't you feel ashamed to be got up like a bogeyman?

Voice. How dare you!

Nandini. Those whom you have scared all along will one day feel ashamed to be afraid. If my Rañjan were here, he would have snapped his fingers in your face, and not been afraid even if he died for it.

Voice. Your impudence is something great. I should like to stand you up on the top of a heap of everything I've smashed throughout my life. And then—

Nandini. Then what?

Voice. Then, like a squeezed bunch of grapes with its juice running out from between the gripping fingers, if I could but hold you tight with these two hands of mine,—and then—go, go, run away, at once, at once!

Nandini. If you shout at me so rudely, I'll stay on, do what you will!

Voice. I long savagely to prove to you how cruel I am. Have you never heard moans from inside my room?

Nandini. I have. Whose moaning was it?

Voice. The hidden mystery of life, wrenched away by me, bewails its torn ties. To get fire from a tree you have to burn it. Nandini, there is fire within you too, red fire. One day I shall burn you and extract that also.

Nandini. Oh, you are cruel!

Voice. I must either gather or scatter. I can feel no pity for what I do not get. Breaking is a fierce kind of getting.

Nandini. But why thrust out your clenched fist like that?

Voice. Here, I take away my fist. Now fly, as the dove flies from the shadow of a hawk.

Nandini. Very well, I will go, and not vex you any more.

Voice. Here, listen, come back, Nandini!

Nandini. What is it?

Voice. On your face, there is the play of life in your eyes and lips; at the back of you flows your black hair, the silent fall of death. The other day when my hands sank into it they felt the *soft calm of dying.* I long to sleep with my face hidden inside those thick black clusters. You don't know how tired I am!

Nandini. Don't you ever sleep?

Voice. I feel afraid to sleep.

Nandini. Let me sing you the latest song that I've learnt.

[*Sings.*]

'I love, I love' is the cry that breaks out from
the bosom of earth and water.
The sky broods like an aching heart, the horizon is
tender like eyes misted with tears.

Voice. Enough! Enough! stop your singing!

Nandini [*sings on*].

A lament heaves and bursts
on the shore of the sea.
The whispers of forgotten days
are born in new leaves to die again.

See, Bishu, he has left the dead frog there and disappeared. He is afraid of songs.

Bishu. The old frog in his heart yearns to die when it hears singing, that's why he feels afraid. My mad girl, why is there a strange light on your face to-day, like the glow of a distant torch in the sky?

Nandini. News has reached me, Rañjan is coming to-day.

Bishu. How?

Nandini. Let me tell you. Every day a pair of blue-throats come and sit on the pomegranate tree in front of my window. Every night, before I sleep, I salute the pole star and say: Sacred star of constancy, if a feather from the wings of the blue-throats finds its way into my room, then I will know my Rañjan is coming. This morning, as soon as I woke, I found a feather on my bed. See, here it is under my breast-cloth. When I meet him I shall put this feather on his crest.

Bishu. They say blue-throats' wings are an omen of victory.

Nandini. Rañjan's way to victory lies through my heart.

Bishu. No more of this; let me go to my work.

Nandini. I shan't let you work to-day.

Bishu. What must I do then.

Nandini. Sing that song of waiting.

Bishu [*sings*].

He who ever wants me through the ages,—
is it not he who sits to-day by my wayside?
I seem to remember a glimpse I had of his face,
in the twilight dusk of some ancient year.
Is it not he who sits to-day by the wayside?

Nandini. Bishu, when you sing I cannot help feeling that I owe you much, but have never given anything to you.

Bishu. I shall decorate my forehead with the mark of your never-giving, and go my way. No little-giving for me, in return for my song! Where will you go now?

Nandini. To the wayside by which Rañjan is coming.

[*They go.*]

[*The* Governor *and a* Headman *come in.*]

Governor. No, we can't possibly allow Rañjan to enter this parish.

Headman. I put him to work in the tunnels of Vajragarh.

Governor. Well, what happened?

Headman. He said he was not used to being made to work. The Headman of Vajragarh came with the police, but the fellow doesn't know what fear is. Threaten him, he bursts out laughing. Asked why he laughs, he says solemnity is the mask of stupidity and he has come to take it off.

Governor. Did you set him to work with the diggers?

Headman. I did, I thought that pressure would make him yield. But on the contrary it seemed to lift the pressure from the diggers' minds also. He cheered them up, and asked them to have a digger's dance!

Governor. Digger's dance! What on earth is that?

Headman. Rañjan started singing. Where were they to get drums?—they objected. Rañjan said, if there weren't any drums, there were spades enough. So they began keeping time with the spades, making a joke of their digging up of nuggets.

The Headman himself came over to reprimand them. 'What style of work is this?' he thundered.
'I have unbound the work,' said Rañjan. 'It won't have to be dragged out by main force any more, it will run along of itself, dancing.'

Governor. The fellow is mad, I see.

Headman. Hopelessly mad. 'Use your spade properly,' shouted I. 'Much better give me a guitar,' said he, smiling.

Governor. But how did he manage to escape from Vajragarh and come up here?

Headman. That I do not know. Nothing seems to fasten on to him. His boisterousness is infectious. The diggers are getting frisky.

Governor. Hallo, isn't that Rañjan himself,—going along the road, thrumming on an old guitar? Impudent rascal! He doesn't even care to hide.

Headman. Well, I never! Goodness alone knows how he broke through the wall!

Governor. Go and seize him instantly! He must not meet Nandini in this parish, for anything.

[*Enters* Assistant Governor.]

Governor. Where are you going?

Assistant Governor. To arrest Rañjan.

Governor. Where is the Deputy Governor?

Assistant Governor. He is so much amused by this fellow that he doesn't want to lay hands on him. He says the man's laugh shows us what queer creatures we governors have grown into.

Governor. I have an idea. Don't arrest Rañjan. Send him on to the King's sanctum.

Assistant Governor. He refuses to obey our call, even in the King's name.

Governor. Tell him the King has made a slave-girl of his Nandini.

Assistant Governor. But if the King—

Governor. Don't you worry. Come on, I'll go with you myself.

[*They go.*]

[*Enter* Professor *and* Antiquarian.]

Antiquarian. I say, what is this infernal noise going on inside?

Professor. The King, probably in a temper with himself, is engaged in breaking some of his own handiwork.

Antiquarian. It sounds like big pillars crashing down one after another.

Professor. There was a lake, at the foot of our hill over there, in which the waters of this Sankhini river used to gather. One day, suddenly, the rock to its left gave way, and the stored-up water rushed out laughing like mad. To see the King now-a-days, it strikes me that his treasure lake has grown weary of its rock wall.

Antiquarian. What did you bring me here for, Professor?

Professor. Latterly he has begun to get angry with my science. He says it only burgles through one wall to reveal another behind it, and never reaches the inner chamber of the Life spirit. I thought that, perhaps in the study of antiquity, he might explore the secret of Life's play. My knapsack has been rifled empty, now he can go on pocket-picking history.

Antiquarian. A girl wearing a grass-green robe.

Professor. She has for her mantle the green joy of the earth. That is our Nandini. In this Yaksha Town there are governors, foremen, headmen, tunnel-diggers, scholars like myself; there are policemen, executioners, and undertakers,—altogether a beautiful assortment! Only *she* is out of element. Midst the clamour of the market place she is a tuned-up lyre. There are days when the mesh of my studies is torn by the sudden breeze of her passing by, and through that rent my attention flies away *swish,* like a bird.

Antiquarian. Good heavens, man! Are even your well-seasoned bones subject to these poetic fits?

Professor. Life's attraction, like the tidal wave, tears away mind from its anchorage of books.

Antiquarian. Tell me, where am I to meet the King.

Professor. There's no means of meeting him. You'll have to talk to him from outside this network.

Antiquarian. We're to converse with this net between us?

Professor. Not the kind of whispered talk that may take place through a woman's veil, but solidly concentrated conversation. Even the cows in his stall don't dare to give milk, they yield their butter straight off.

Antiquarian. Admirable! To extract the essential from the diluted, is what scholars aim at.

Professor. But not what God in His creation aims at. He respects the fruit stones that are hard, but rejoices in the pulp that is sweet.

Antiquarian. Professor, I see that your grey science is galloping fast towards grass-green. But I wonder how you can stand this King of yours.

Professor. Shall I tell you the truth? I love him.

Antiquarian. You don't mean to say so?

Professor. He is so great that even what is wrong with him will not be able to spoil him.

[*The* Governor *comes in.*]

Governor. I say, man of science, so this is the person you volunteered to bring here. Our King flew into a passion at the very mention of his special subject.

Antiquarian. May I ask why?

Governor. The King says there is no age of history which may be called old. It is always an eternal extension of the present.

Antiquarian. Can the front exist without the back?

Governor. What he said was: 'Time proceeds by revealing the new on his front; but the men of learning, suppressing that fact, will have it that Time ever carries the burden of the old on his back.'

[Nandini *comes in hurriedly.*]

Nandini. What is happening? Who are they?

Governor. Hallo, Nandini, is that you? I shall wear your *kunda* chain late in the evening. When three-quarters of me can hardly be seen for the dark, then perchance a flower garland might become even me.

Nandini. Look over there—what a piteous sight! Who are those people, going along with the guards, filing out from the backdoor of the King's apartments?

Governor. We call them the King's leavings.

Nandini. What does that mean?

Governor. Some day you too will know its meaning; let it be for today.

Nandini. But are these men? Have they flesh and marrow, life and soul?

Governor. Maybe they haven't.

Nandini. Had they never any?

Governor. Maybe they had.

Nandini. Where then is it all gone now?

Governor. Man of science, explain it if you can, I'm off.

[*He goes.*]

Nandini. Alas, alas! I see amongst these shadows faces that I know. Surely that is our Anup and Upamanyu?

Professor, they belong to our neighbouring village. Two brothers as tall as they were strong. They used to come and race their boats in our river on the fourteenth day of the moon in rainy June. Oh, who has brought them to this miserable plight?

See, there goes Shaklu,—in sword play he used to win the prize garland before all the others. Anu-up! Sha-klu-u! look this way; it's I, your the principle underlying all rise to greatness.

Nandini. It's a fiendish principle!

Professor. It's no use getting annoyed with a principle. Principles are neither good nor bad. That which happens *does* happen. To go against it, is to knock your head against the law of being.

Nandini. If this is the way of man's being, I refuse to *be*, I want to depart with those shadows,—show me the way.

Professor. When the time comes for showing us out, the great ones themselves will point the way. Before that, there's no such nuisance as a way at all! You see how our Antiquarian has quietly slipped off, thinking he'll fly and save himself. After going a few steps, he'll soon discover that there's a wire network stretched from post to post, from country to country.

Nandini, I see, your temper is rising. The red oleanders against your flaming cheek are beginning to look like evening storm clouds gathering for a night of terror.

Nandini [*knocking at the net window*]. Listen, listen!

Professor. Whom are you calling?

Nandini. That King of yours, shrouded in his mist of netting.

Professor. The door of the inner room has been closed. He won't hear you.

Nandini [*calling out*]. Bishu, mad brother mine!

Professor. What d'you want with *him?*

Nandini. Why hasn't he come back yet? I feel afraid.

Professor. He was with you only a little while ago.

Nandini. The Governor said he was wanted to identify Rañjan. I tried to go with him, but they wouldn't let me. Whose groaning is that?

Professor. It must be that wrestler of ours.

Nandini. What wrestler?

Professor. The world-famous Gajju, whose brother, Bhajan, had the bravado to challenge the King to a wrestling match, since when not even a thread of his loin cloth is anywhere to be seen. That put Gajju on his mettle, and he came on with great sound and fury. I told him at the outset that, if he wanted to dig in the tunnels underneath this kingdom, he was welcome,—he could at least drag on a dead and alive existence for some time. But if he wanted to make a show of heroics, that would not be tolerated for a moment.

Nandini. Does it at all make for their well-being thus to keep watch and ward over these man-traps night and day?

Professor. Well-being! There's no question of 'well' in it at all,—only 'being'. That *being* of theirs has expanded so terribly that, unless millions of men are pressed into service, who's going to support its weight? So the net is spreading farther and farther. They must exist, you see.

Nandini. Must they? If it is necessary to die in order to live like men, what harm in dying?

Professor. Again that anger, the wild cry of red oleander? It is sweet, no doubt, yet what is true is true. If it gives you pleasure to say that one must die to live, well, say so by all means; but those who say that others must die that they themselves may live,—it's only they who are actually alive. You may cry out that this shows a lack of humanity, but you forget, in your indignation, that this is what humanity itself happens to be. The tiger does not feed on the tiger, it's only man who fattens on his fellow-man.

[*The* Wrestler *totters in.*]

Nandini. Oh poor thing, see how he comes, staggering. Wrestler, lie down here. Professor, do see where he's hurt.

Professor. You won't see any outward sign of a wound.

Wrestler. All-merciful God, grant me strength once more in my life, if only for one little day!

Professor. Why, my dear fellow?

Wrestler. Just to wring that Governor's neck!

Professor. What has the Governor done to you?

Wrestler. It's he who brought about the whole thing. I never wanted to fight. Now, after egging me on, he goes about saying it's my fault.

Professor. Why, what interest had he in your fighting?

Wrestler. They only feel safe when they rob the whole world of strength. Lord of Mercy, grant that I may be able to gouge his eyes out some day, to tear asunder his lying tongue!

Nandini. How do you feel now, Wrestler?

Wrestler. Altogether hollowed out! These demons know the magic art of sucking away not only strength but hope.

If only once I could somehow,—O good God, but once,—everything is possible to Thy mercy,—if only I could fasten my teeth for once in the Governor's throat!

Nandini. Professor, help me to raise him.

Professor. That would be a crime, Nandini, according to the custom of this land.

Nandini. Wouldn't it be a crime to let the man perish?

Professor. That which there is none to punish may be a sin, but never a crime. Nandini, come away, come right away out of this. The tree spreads its root-fingers and does its grabbing underground, but there it does not bring forth its flowers. Flowers bloom on the branches which reach towards the light. My sweet Red Oleander, don't try to probe our secrets in the depths of their dust. Be for us swaying in the air above, that we may gaze upwards to see you.

There comes the Governor. He hates to see me talk to you. So I must go.

Nandini. Why is he so dead against me?

Professor. I can guess. You have touched his heart-strings. The longer it takes to tune them up, the more awful the discord meanwhile.

[*The* Professor *goes, the* Governor *comes in.*]

Nandini. Sir Governor!

Governor. Nandini, when our Gosain saw that *kunda* garland of yours in my room, both his eyes,—but here he comes— [*The* Gosain *comes in.*]

Your Holiness, accept my reverence. That garland was given to me by our Nandini here.

Gosain. Ah indeed! the gift of a pure heart! God's own white *kunda* flowers! Their beauty remains unsullied even in the hands of a man of the world. This is what gives one faith in the power of virtue, and hope for the sinners' redemption.

Nandini. Please do something for this man, Your Reverence. There's very little life left in him.

Gosain. The Governor is sure to keep him as much alive as it is necessary for him to be. But, my child, these discussions will become your lips.

Nandini. So in this kingdom you follow some calculation in apportioning life?

Gosain. Of course,—for mortal life has its limits. Our class of people have their great burden to bear, therefore we have to claim a larger portion of life's sustenance for our share. That's according to Almighty God's own decree.

Nandini. Reverend Sir, may I know what good God has so heavily charged you to do to these people?

Gosain. The life that is unlimited gives no provocation to fight for its distribution. We Preachers have the charge of turning these people towards this unlimited life. So long as they remain content with that, we are their friends.

Nandini. Let me come over to the Headman's quarters to help you.

Wrestler. No. Don't add to my troubles, I beg of you.

[*The* Wrestler *goes.*]

Nandini. Governor, stay, tell me, whither have you taken my Bishu?

Governor. Who am I that I should take him? The wind carries off the clouds,—if you think that to be a crime, make enquiries as to who is behind the wind.

Nandini. Dear me, what an awful place! You are not men, and those you drive are not men, either,—you are winds and they are clouds!

Reverend Gosain, I am sure, *you* know where my Bishu is.

Gosain. I know, for sure, that wherever he is, it's for the best.

Nandini. For whose best?

Gosain. That you won't understand—

Oh, I say, leave off, let go of that, it's my rosary.—Hallo, Governor, what wild girl is this you have—

Governor. The girl has somehow managed to ensconce herself in a niche, safe from the laws of this land, and we can't lay hands on her. Our King himself—

Gosain. Good heavens, now she'll tear off my wrap of the Holy Name too. What unspeakable outrage!

[*The* Gosain *flies.*]

Nandini. Governor, you *must* tell me where you have taken Bishu.

Governor. They have summoned him to the court of judgement. That's all that there is to tell you. Let me go.

Nandini. Because I am a woman, you are not afraid of me? God sends His thunderbolt through His messenger, the lightning spark—that bolt I have borne here with me; it will shatter the golden spire of your mastery.

Governor. Then let me tell you the truth before I go. It's you who have dragged Bishu into danger.

Nandini. I?

Governor. Yes, you! He was so long content to be quietly burrowing away underground like a worm. It's you who taught him to spread the wings of death. O fire of the gods, you'll yet draw forth many more to their fate.—Then at length will you and I come to our understanding, and that won't be long.

Nandini. So may it be. But tell me one thing before you go. Will you not let Rañjan come and see me?

Governor. No, never.

Nandini. Never, you say! I defy you to do your worst. This very day I am sure, absolutely sure, that he and I will meet!

[Governor *goes.*]

Nandini [*knocking and tugging at the network*]. Listen, listen, King! Where's your court of judgement? Open its door to me. [Kishôr *comes in.*]

Who is that? My boy, Kishôr! Do you know where Bishu is?

Kishôr. Yes, Nandini, be ready to see him. I don't know how it was, the Chief of the Guard took a fancy to my youthfulness and yielded to my entreaties. He has consented to take him along by this path.

Nandini. Guard! Take him along? Is he then—

Kishôr. Yes, here they come.

Nandini. What! Handcuffs on your wrists? Friend of my heart, where are they taking you like that?

[Bishu *comes in under arrest.*]

Bishu. It's nothing to be anxious about!—Guards, please wait a little, let me say a few words to her.—My wild girl, my heart's joy, at last I am free.

Nandini. What do you mean, Singer of my heart? I don't understand your words.

Bishu. When I used to be afraid, and try to avoid danger at every step, I seemed to be at liberty; but that liberty was the worst form of bondage.

Nandini. What offence have you committed that they should take you away thus?

Bishu. I spoke out the truth to-day, at last.

Nandini. What if you did?

Bishu. No harm at all!

Nandini. Then why did they bind you like this?

Bishu. What harm in that either? These chains will bear witness to the truth of my freedom.

Nandini. Don't they feel ashamed of themselves to lead you along the road chained like a beast? Aren't they men too?

Bishu. They have a big beast inside them, that's why their heads are not lowered by the indignity of man, rather the inner brute's tail swells and wags with pride at man's downfall.

Nandini. O dear heart! Have they been hurting you? What are these marks on your body?

Bishu. They have whipped me, with the whips they use for their dogs. The string of that whip is made with the same thread which goes to the stringing of their Gosain's rosary. When they tell their beads they don' t remember that; but probably their God is aware of it.

Nandini. Let them bind me like that too, and take me away with you, my heart's joy! Unless I share some of your punishment I shan't be able to touch food from to-day.

Kishôr. I'm sure I can persuade them to take me in exchange for you. Let me take your place, Bishu.

Bishu. Don't be silly!

Kishôr. Punishment won't hurt me. I am young. I shall bear it with joy.

Nandini. No, no, do not talk like that.

Kishôr. Nandini, my absence has been noticed, their bloodhounds are after me. Allow me to escape the indignity awaiting me by taking shelter in a punishment I joyfully accept.

Bishu. No, it won't do for you to be caught—not for a while yet. There's work for you, dear boy, and dangerous work too. Rañjan has come. You must find him out.

Kishôr. Then I bid you farewell, Nandini. What is your message when I meet Rañjan?

Nandini. This tassel of red oleanders. [*Hands it to him.*]

[Kishôr *goes.*]

Bishu. May you both be united once again.

Nandini. That union will give me no pleasure now. I shall never be able to forget that I sent you away empty-handed. And what has that poor boy, Kishôr, got from me?

Bishu. All the treasure hidden in his heart has been revealed to him by the fire you have lighted in his life. Nandini, I remind you, it's for you to put that blue-throat's feather on Rañjan's crest.—There, do you hear them singing the harvest song?

Nandini. I do, and it wrings my heart, to tears.

Bishu. The play of the fields is ended now, and the field-master is taking the ripe corn home. Come on, Guards, let's not linger anymore. [*Sings.*]

Mow the corn of the last harvest,
bind it in sheaves.
The remainder, let it return
as dust unto the dust.

[*They go.*]

[*The* Governor *and a* Doctor *come in.*]

Doctor. I've seen him. I find the King.

Governor. My wife will be driving out to-day. The post will be changed near your village, and you must see that she's not detained.

Headman. There's a plague on the cattle of our parish, and not a single ox can be had to draw the car. Never mind, we can press the diggers into service.

Governor. You know where you have to take her? To the garden-house, where the feast of the Flag-worship is to be held.

Headman. I'll see to it at once, but let me tell you one thing before I go. That 69 Ng, whom they call mad Bishu,—it's high time to cure his madness.

Governor. Why, how does he annoy you?

Headman. Not so much by what he says or does, as by what he implies.

Governor. There's no need to worry about him any further. You understand!

Headman. Really! That's good news, indeed! Another thing. That 47 V, he's rather too friendly with 69 Ng.

Governor. I have observed that.

Headman. Your Lordship's observation is ever keen. Only, as you have to keep an eye on so many things, one or two may perchance escape your notice. For instance, there's our No. 95, a distant connection of mine by marriage, ever ready to make sandals for the feet of Your Lordship's sweeper out of his own ribs,—so irrepressibly loyal is he that even his wife hangs her head for very shame,—and yet up to now—

Governor. His name has been entered in the High Register.

Headman. Ah, then his lifelong service will at last receive its reward! The news must be broken to him gently, because he gets epileptic fits, and supposing suddenly—

Governor. All right, we'll see to that. Now be off, there's no time.

Headman. Just a word about another person,—though he's my own brother-in-law. When his mother died, my wife brought him up with her own hands; yet for my master's sake—

Governor. You can tell me about him another time. Run away now.

Headman. There comes His Honour the Deputy Governor. Please speak a word to him on my behalf. He doesn't look upon me with favour. I suspect that when 69 Ng used to enjoy the favour of free entry into the palace, he must have been saying things against me.

Governor. I assure you, he never even mentioned your name.

Headman. That's just his cleverness! What can be more damaging than to suppress the name of a man, whose name is his best asset? These schemers have their different ways. No. 33 of our parish has an incurable habit of haunting Your Lordship's private chamber. One is always afraid of his inventing goodness knows what calumnies about other people. And yet if one knew the truth about his own—

Governor. There's positively no time to-day. Get away with you, quick!

Headman. I make my salute. [*Coming back.*] Just one word more lest I forget. No. 88 of our neighbouring parish started work on a miserable pittance, and before two years are out his income has run into thousands, not to speak of extras! Your Lordship's mind is like that of the gods—a few words of hypocritical praise are enough to draw down the best of your boons.

Governor. All right, all right,—that can keep for to-morrow.

Headman. I'm not so mean as to suggest taking away the bread from his mouth. But Your Lordship should seriously consider whether it's wise to keep him on at the Treasury. Our Vishnu Dutt knows him inside out. If you send—

Governor. I shall send for him this very day. But begone,—not another word!

Headman. Your Lordship, my third son is getting to be quite a big boy. He came the other day to prostrate himself at your feet. After two days of dancing attendance outside, he had to go away without gaining admission to you. He feels it very bitterly. My daughter-in-law has made with her own hands an offering of sweet pumpkin for Your Lordship—

Governor. Oh confound you! Tell him to come day after to-morrow, he will be admitted. *Now, will you—*

[Headman *goes. The* Deputy Governor *comes in.*]

Deputy Governor. I've just sent on the dancing girls and musicians to the garden.

Governor. And that little matter about Rañjan,—how far—?

Deputy Governor. That kind of work is not in my line. The Assistant Governor has taken it upon himself to do the job. By this time his—

Governor. Does the King—?

Deputy Governor. The King can't possibly have understood. Some lie told by our men has goaded Rañjan to frenzy, and he's rushing to the usual fate of—I detest the whole business. Moreover, I don't think it right to deceive the King like this.

Governor. That responsibility is mine. Now then, that girl must be—

Deputy Governor. Don't talk of all that to me. The Headman who has been put on duty is the right man,—he doesn't stick at any dirtiness whatever.

Governor. Does that man Gosain know about this affair?

Deputy Governor. I'm sure he can guess, but he's careful not to know for certain.

Governor. What's his object?

Deputy Governor. For fear of there being no way left open for saying: 'I don't believe it.'

Governor. But what makes him take all this trouble?

Deputy Governor. Don't you see? The poor man is really two in one, clumsily joined,—Priest on the skin, Governor at the marrow. He has to take precious care to prevent the Governor part of him coming up to the surface, lest it should clash too much with his telling of beads.

Governor. He might have dropped the beads altogether.

Deputy Governor. No, for whatever his blood may be, his mind, in a sense, is really pious. If only he can tell his beads in his temple, and revel in slave-driving in his dreams, he feels happy. But for him, the true complexion of our God would appear too black. In fact, Gosain is placed here only to help our God to feel comfortable.

Governor. My friend, I see the instinct of the Ruler doesn't seem to match with the colour of your own blood, either!

Deputy Governor. There's hope still. Human blood is fast drying up. But I can't stomach your No. 321 yet. When I'm obliged to embrace him in public, no holy water seems able to wash out the impurity of his touch.

[*Here comes* Nandini.]

Governor. Come away, I don't trust you. I know the spell of Nandini has fallen on your eyes.

Deputy Governor. I know that as well as you do. But you don't seem to know that a tinge of her oleanders has got mixed with the colour of duty in *your* eyes too—that's what makes them so frightfully red.

Governor. That may be. Fortunately for us, our mind knows not its own secret. Come away. [*They go.*]

[Nandini *comes in.*]

Nandini [*knocking and pushing at the network*]. Listen, listen, listen!

[Gosain *comes in.*]

Gosain. Whom are you prodding like that?

Nandini. That boa-constrictor of yours, who remains in hiding and swallows men.

Gosain. Lord, lord! When Providence wishes to destroy the small, it does so by putting big words into their little mouths.

See here, Nandini, believe me when I tell you that I aim at your welfare.

Nandini. Try some more real method of doing me good.

Gosain. Come to my sanctuary, let me chant you the Holy Name for a while.

Nandini. What have I to do with the name?

Gosain. You will gain peace of mind.

Nandini. Shame, shame on me if I do! I shall sit and wait here at the door.

Gosain. You have more faith in men than in God?

Nandini. Your God of the Flagstaff,—he will never unbend. But the man who is lost to sight behind the netting, will he also remain bound in his network for ever? Go, go. It's your trade to delude men with words, after filching away their lives. [Gosain *goes.*]

[*Enter* Phágulal *and* Chandrá.]

Phágulal. Our Bishu came away with you, where is he now? Tell us the truth.

Nandini. He has been made prisoner and taken away.

Chandrá. You witch, you must have given information against him. You are their spy.

Nandini. You don't really believe that!

Chandrá. What else are you doing here?

Phágulal. Every person suspects every other person in this cursed place. Yet I have always trusted you, Nandini. In my heart I used to—However, let that pass. But to-day it looks very very strange, I must say.

Nandini. Perhaps it does. It may really be even as you say. Bishu has got into trouble for coming with me. He used to be quite safe in your company, he said so himself.

Chandrá. Then why did you decoy him away, you evil-omened creature?

Nandini. Because he said he wanted to be free.

Chandrá. A precious kind of freedom you have given him!

Nandini. I could not understand all that he said, Chandrá. Why did he tell me that freedom could only be found by plunging down to the bottom of danger?—Phágulal, how could I save him who wanted to be free from the tyranny of safety?

Chandrá. We don't understand all this. If you can't bring him back, you'll have to pay for it. I'm not to be taken in by that coquettish prettiness of yours.

Phágulal. What's the use of idle bickering? Let's gather a big crowd from the workmen's lines, and then go and smash the prison gate.

Nandini. I'll come with you.

Phágulal. What for?

Nandini. To join in the breaking.

Chandrá. As if you haven't done quite enough breaking already, you sorceress!

[Gôkul *comes in.*]

Gôkul. That witch must be burnt alive, before everything else.

Chandrá. That won't be punishment enough. First knock off that beauty of hers, with which she goes about ruining people. Weed it out of her face as the grass is weeded with a hoe.

Gôkul. That I can do. Let this hammer just have a dance on her nose tip—

Phágulal. Beware! If you dare touch her—

Nandini. Stop, Phágulal. He's coward; he wants to strike me because he's afraid of me. I don't fear his blows one bit.

Gôkul. Phágulal, you haven't come to your senses yet. You think the Governor alone is your enemy. Well, I admire a straightforward enemy. But that sweet-mouthed beauty of yours—

Nandini. Ah, so you too admire the Governor, as the mud beneath his feet admires the soles of his shoes!

Phágulal. Gôkul, the time has at length come to show your prowess, but not by fighting a girl. Come along with me. I'll show you what to fight.

[Phágulal, Chandrá, *and* Gôkul *go.*]

[*A band of* Men *come in.*]

Nandini. Where are you going, my good men?

First Man. We carry the offering for the Flag-worship.

Nandini. Have you seen Rañjan?

Second Man. I saw him once, five days ago, but not since. Ask those others who follow us.

Nandini. Who are they?

Third Man. They are bearing wine for the Governors' feast.

[*The first batch goes, another comes in.*]

Nandini. Look here, red-caps, have you seen Rañjan?

First Man. I saw him the other day at the house of Headman Sambhu.

Nandini. Where is he now?

Second Man. D'you see those men taking the ladies' dresses for the feast? Ask them. They hear a lot of things that don't reach our ears.

[*Second batch goes, a third come in.*]

Nandini. Do *you* know, my men, where they have kept Rañjan?

First Man. Hush, hush!

Nandini. I am sure you know. You *must* tell me.

Second Man. What enters by our ears doesn't come out by our mouths, that's why we are still alive. Ask one of the men who are carrying the weapons.

[*They go, others come in.*]

Nandini. Oh do stop a moment and listen to me. Tell me, where is Rañjan?

First Man. The auspicious hour draws near. It's time for the King himself to come for the Flag-worship. Ask him about it when he steps out. We only know the beginning, not the end. [*They go.*]

Nandini [*shaking the network violently*]. Open the door. The time has come.

Voice [*behind the scenes*]. But not for you. Go away from here.

Nandini. You must hear *now* what I have to say. It cannot wait for another time.

Voice. You want Rañjan, I know. I have asked the Governor to fetch him at once. But don't remain standing at the door when I come out for the worship, for then you'll run great risk.

Nandini. I have cast away all fear. You can't drive me away. Happen what may, I'm not going to move till your door is opened.

Voice. To-day's for the Flag-worship. Don't distract my mind. Get away from my door.

Nandini. The gods have all eternity for their worship, they're not pressed for time. But the sorrows of men cannot wait.

King. Deceived! These traitors have deceived me,—perdition take them! My own machine refuses my sway! Call the Governor—bring him to me handcuffed—

Nandini. King, they all say you know magic. Make him wake up for my sake.

King. My magic can only put an end to waking.—Alas! I know not how to awaken.

Nandini. Then lull me to sleep,—the same sleep! Oh, why did you work this havoc? I cannot bear it any more.

King. I have killed youth. Yes, I have indeed killed youth,—all these years, with all my strength. The curse of youth, dead, is upon me.

Nandini. Did he not take my name?

King. He did,—in such a way that every vein in my body was set on fire.

Nandini [*to* Rañjan]. My love, my brave one, here do I place this blue-throat's feather in your crest. Your victory has begun from today, and I am its bearer. Ah, here is that tassel of my flowers in his hand. Then Kishôr must have met him—

But where is he? King, where is that boy?

King. Which boy?

Nandini. The boy who brought these flowers to Rañjan.

King. That absurd little child! He came to defy me with his girlish face.

Nandini. And then? Tell me! Quick!

King. He burst himself against me, like a bubble.

Nandini. King, the Time is indeed now come!

King. Time for what?

Nandini. For the last fight between you and me.

King. But I can kill you in no time,—this instant.

Nandini. From that very instant that death of mine will go on killing you every single moment.

King. Be brave, Nandini, trust me. Make me your comrade to-day.

Nandini. What would you have me do?

King. To fight against me, but with your hand in mine. That fight has already begun. There is my flag. First I break the Flagstaff,—thus! Next it's for you to tear its banner. Let your hand unite with mine to kill me, utterly kill me. That will be my emancipation.

Guards [*rushing up*]. What are you doing, King? You dare break the Flagstaff, the holiest symbol of our divinity? The Flagstaff which has its one point piercing the heart of the earth and the other that of heaven! What a terrible sin,—on the very day of the Flag-worship! Comrades, let us go and inform our Governors. [*They run off.*]

King. A great deal of breaking remains to be done. You will come with me, Nandini?

Nandini. I will.

[Phágulal *comes in.*]

Phágulal. They won't hear of letting Bishu off. I am afraid, they'll—Who is this? The King!

Oh you wicked witch,—conspiring with the King himself! O vile deceiver!

King. What is the matter with you? What is that crowd out for?

Phágulal. To break the prison gate. We may lose our lives, but we shan't fall back.

King. Why should you fall back? I too am out for breaking. Behold the first sign—my broken Flagstaff!

Phágulal. What! This is altogether beyond us simple folk.

Be merciful, Nandini, don't deceive me. Am I to believe my eyes?

Nandini. Brother, you have set out to win death. You have left no chance for deception to touch you.

Phágulal. You too come along with us, our own Nandini!

Nandini. That is what I'm still alive for, Phágulal. I wanted to bring my Rañjan amongst you. Look there, he has come, my hero, braving death!

Phágulal. Oh, horror! Is that Rañjan lying there, silent?

Nandini. Not silent. He leaves behind him in death his conquering call. He will live again, he cannot die.

Phágulal. Ah, my Nandini, my beautiful one, was it for this you were waiting all these eager days?

Nandini. I *did* await his coming, and he *did* come. I still wait to prepare for his coming again, and he *shall* come again. Where is Chandrá?

Phágulal. She has gone with her tears and prayers to the Governor, accompanied by Gôkul. I'm afraid Gôkul is seeking to take up service with the Governor. He will betray us.

King, are you sure you don't mistake us? We are out to break your own prison, I tell you!

King. Yes, it is my *own* prison. You and I must work together, for you cannot break it alone.

Phágulal. As soon as the Governor hears of it, he will march with all his forces to prevent us.

King. Yes, my fight is against them.

Phágulal. But the soldiers will not obey you.

King. You will be on my side!

Phágulal. Shall we be able to win through?

King. We shall at least be able to die! At last I have found the meaning of death. I am saved!

Phágulal. King, do you hear the tumult?

King. There comes the Governor with his troops. How could he be so quick about it? He must have been prepared beforehand. They have used my own power against me.

Phágulal. My men have not yet turned up.

King. They will never come. The Governor is sure to get round them.

Nandini. I had my last hope that they would bring my Bishu to me. Will that never be?

King. No hope of that, I'm afraid.

Phágulal. Then come along, Nandini, let us take you to a safe place first. The Governor will see red, if he but catches sight of you.

Nandini. You want to banish me into the solitary exile of safety? [*Calling out*] Governor! Governor!—He has swung up my garland of *kunda* flowers on his spear-head. I will dye that garland the colour of my oleanders with my heart's blood.—Governor! He has seen me! Victory to Rañjan! [*Runs off.*]

King [*calling after her*]. Nandini! [*Follows her.*]

[*The* Professor *comes in.*]

Phágulal. Where are *you* hurrying to, Professor?

Professor. Some one said that the King has at last had tidings of the secret of Life, and has gone off in quest of it. I have thrown away my books to follow him.

Phágulal. The King has just gone off to his death. He has heard Nandini's call.

Professor. The network is torn to shreds! Where is Nandini?

Phágulal. She has gone before them all. We can't reach her any more.

Professor. It is only now that we shall reach her. She won't evade us any longer.

[Professor *rushes out,* Bishu *comes in.*]

Bishu. Phágulal, where is Nandini?

Phágulal. How did you get here?

Bishu. Our workmen have broken into the prison. There they are,—running off to fight. I came to look for Nandini. Where is she?

Phágulal. She has gone in advance of us all.

Bishu. Where?

Phágulal. To the last freedom. Bishu, do you see who is lying there?

Bishu. Rañjan!

Phágulal. You see the red streak?

Bishu. I understand,—then red marriage.

Phágulal. They are united.

Bishu. Now it is for me to take my last lonely journey.—Perhaps we may meet.—Perhaps she may want me to sing.—My mad girl, O my mad girl!—

Come, brother, on to the fight!

Phágulal. To the fight! Victory to Nandini!

Bishu. Victory to Nandini!

Phágulal. Here is her wristlet of red oleanders. She has bared her arm to-day,—and left us.

Bishu. Once I told her I would not take anything from her hand. I break my word and take this. Come along!

[*They go.*]

[*Song in the distance.*]

Hark 'tis Autumn calling,—
Come, O come away!
The earth's mantle of dust is filled with ripe corn!
O the joy! the joy!

Reference

English Writings of Tagore, Vol. 3, New Delhi: Atlantic Publishers and Distributors (P) Ltd., 2007, pp. 211-65

APPENDICES

Appendix I

Tagore on Red Oleanders[1]

'Red Oleanders: An Interpretation'

For those of us who are concerned with life and with the play of human forces across the stage of our daily existence, it is the underlying significance which forms the kernel of the problem. In this play there is no attempt to point a moral or to preach a sermon, but because these characters "are the abstract and brief chronicles of the time", they give us a mirror in which perhaps we may catch some glimpse of that truth to which we are so accustomed that we have forgotten all about it. The test of every great work of art, in colour, sound, form or word, is this test of significance. The artist has had something great to say and he has said it greatly, so truth is revealed. But to do this, and much modern work shows a woeful lack of consciousness in the matter, life itself must be a great work of art, so that out of significance of his life a man will draw forth that which holds the essence of truth and, with the tool over which he has the most complete mastery, will give to it artistic shape. There are those who, in perfecting their tool of craftsmanship, spend their whole lives comparing their facility of use with that of others and await with anxiety the plaudits or criticisms of their fellow craftsmen. This is not so with him who lives greatly. Out of the wealth of his experience of life and of his conviction of truth he draws that which is most truly significant and offers it to us chiseled with no doubting hand and illuminated by his own creative imagination.

In daring to sit in judgment upon *Red Oleanders*, we are not judges, we are the accused. For we stand in front of a great life, the life of one who has lived and drunk of the draft of life from foam to dregs, so that according to our judgment we shall stand judged. The figure on the canvas cannot be separated from its background, else the unity of truth is broken. The background to this play is one which needs careful attention if the characters, as they step upon the stage, are to tell their tale, and keep their significance. Divest them of this and it is so easy to be superficial, to repeat the catchwords of the modern marketplace; a poetic tirade against modern industrialism, the usual hit at Science, the national complain of the subject against oppression. But whether we will or no, the forces that we ordinarily applaud are beaten at the end. They dissolve before the close into a complete insignificance and vanish in the face of a superior force which somehow convinces us, whether we see its significance or not.

In *Red Oleanders*, there are certain underlying principles at work, principles which we can quite easily recognize in our daily existence if we choose to look for one moment under the surface. The habit of greed—greed for things, for power, for facts, with all the ramifications that greed is able to set up between man and man—is arrayed against the explosive force of human sympathy, of neighbourliness, of fellowship and of love, the force which we may term good. Good is here arrayed against the dehumanizing force of mammon, of selfishness, of evil; of that which separates us from our fellows against that which cements us together, of that which, because it divides us, is untruth, is a lie. Only in so far as he recognizes this truth, has man succeeded in reaching the peak upon which the human race now stands, whilst the tiger, a solitary wandering unit, still prowls the jungle alone.

To the gardener of a northern clime the oleander is a flowering shrub, which, because of the character of its foliage and the simple beauty of its red blossoms, well repays careful attention and its place inside the heated greenhouse. In more temperate regions the oleander finds its welcome in the open garden, and will lavish its splendour within the courts of palace or monastery, whilst in India it flourishes of its own accord over jungle and plain. It has the same flower, the same nature, the same principle of growth, but according to temperature and environment it finds devotion from one, appreciation from another, and only cursing and bitterness from the poor cultivator, who, as its roots spread from the hedgerow and invade his scanty plot, must set to work with his *kodali* and root it out. In his struggle for livelihood he is concerned with the underground ramifications of the root system, and with his eyes upon the soil he lacks either time or the energy to glance at the spray of red blossoms that hangs immediately over his head.

Into a world where men have sacrificed every simple human relationship and are grabbing for what they can get, out of each other, out of the soil, out of books or the exploitation of souls, where the beauty of human sympathy is forgotten, the oleander sheds its flower, and, with a shock, some with protest, some in anger, some in response to a deep echo within, cast away their tools and according to their several abilities realize that beauty of life which had dwelt among them, but which they had allowed to grow out of reach.

The background, then, is a world based upon the principle that each must fight the other, oppress or be oppressed, in order not merely that the ordinary simple needs of life may be satisfied, but that piles of accumulation may be set up. This is a world where, with every available means in his power, the Great King exploits the resources of the underworld, of nature, of the mind, of science and of human physique and intelligence, using all the weapons of organization and the elaborate machinery of a highly centralized bureaucracy in order to add to his wealth. This wealth he measures in gold, or in souls or in facts, or in human bodies, so that men are men no longer but numbers. The King sits fascinated as he watches this hive where everyone is busy, but no one content, where all are piling cell to cell, adding honey to honey, guarding the stores of accumulated wealth with efficient death-dealing stings, or casting out the human wastage, the drones, men who have been broken, or exploited. Into his hive flies the butterfly, armed with no sting, equipped with no power to gather or to store, but clothed in beauty, loving the light of day and life, asking all to share in her sunshine revels, kissing one here and one there with the waft of her wings, arousing a petulant anger where others are too busy even to look at her and are annoyed when she interferes with the work in hand. Like strings on an untuned instrument they respond to her touch, and though the instrument had long been thrown on one side, still here and there music and harmony come struggling forth, toils and troubles are forgotten, memories are aroused of the old scents and sounds, of the simple artistic colour and variety of nature, of the co-operative life of the village, where all were not numbers but neighbours, where there was music and beauty of life. But we have become numbers, with numbers on our doors, our telephones, our cars, our factories our restaurants, our votes and our tickets at sports or theatre. Even as worshippers we are card indexed.

Nandini then is this touch of life, the spirit of joy in life. Matched with Ranjan, the spirit of joy in work, together they embody the spirit of love; love in union, union in love, a harmony before which the discord of greed is scattered as under a spell. Linked in this harmony of beauty they walk fearlessly into this world of getting, and, being independent of it, they break down its barriers, even though in the process they are broken themselves,—but such sacrifice is the price which must always be paid in the effort to break down the wall of darkness, of untruth and to flood the world with light. In the face of this combination of simplicity, the king, enclosed in his pride of empire, in his accumulation of wealth, of things, finds a touch of that happiness that he had lost. His gold loses its luster, his scientific experiments, involving the crushing out of human life, and with it of faith and hope, no longer gives him interest. His research into elemental forces, which in his curiosity he has broken down from compounds to molecules, from molecules to atoms, is dazzled and confounded by the beams of a beauty that warms and embraces everything under its cloak of human affection and sympathy.

So it is that, when men make use of men and leave out this elemental touch of kindliness, by which alone we may live in harmony with our surroundings, they crush and mutilate not merely their victims but the humanity which is in themselves. They prefer to think in terms of empire, of organization in factory or field or workshop, in politics or church or sport, and to satisfy their craving for power or survival at the expense of their human feelings. They use every variety of machinery to fortify themselves or their selfish ends against the dissolving power of beauty and love,—the trust, the company, stocks and shares investments, machinery through which they can avoid all human connection and so cut themselves off from their fellows whilst they extract for their own benefit the very essence of the lives of their neighbours. Organizations are set up with the best of aims and ideals and of executive machinery churches, universities, and charitable institutions which, so long as their income is paid regularly, come to depend for their survival upon the denial of just that element of mutual love and trust, sympathy and friendship, which they were pledged to try and establish. In return for the bread of existence they offer a stone, the kind that holds down papers at a meeting of some far-off Board of Directors, and what wonder, when people come to them in their turn for bread, the bread of knowledge or of spiritual refreshment, they only find a stone.

In such organizations men have become mere numbers. The love which is truth and the truth which is love are violated. For to accept in theory the law of love, but to deny it in practice as impracticable today, is not to accept it at all. This is happening wherever men use men as tools, as a means to some further end in which these tools have no part, lot of interest, and where they fail to recognize in their fellow beings a common inheritance of a common humanity.

Through love, the love of a Nandini for a Ranjan, it is possible to accept any gift from man, even his death for your sake. But the moment it becomes necessary for us to depend upon men on any other basis, then it is well for us to walk with caution. We are treading upon holy ground without removing our shoes. Without our knowing what is happening the nails in our shoes grind the life under our feet to dust. We walk rough-shod over our neighbours without realizing that humanity and truth have been violated.

It is to this insensibility and to the growth in size of all ramifications of society that our misery is due. If man were wise he would set to work to discover some common denomination whereby this reduction of life by fractions into death might be prevented for ever. If his intelligence is no longer capable of facing this truth, he must be prepared to face complete entombment and disintegration under the very ramifications which he has himself set up to ward off the day of wrath.

This does not mean that it is necessary for him to cultivate friendship with every individual he meets, but rather that he should extend to all human beings with whom he has any connection, direct or indirect, that same civility and courtesy which he ordinarily reserves for strangers or servants. Civility with friends is not necessary, for, as friendship grows by mutual giving, all barriers break down. Whilst the barrier of strangeness remains, civility or courtesy, is essential. It was this courtesy which made something great of the battles of olden time, but which, now lost, has started the whole human race on a downward path. Once man disdains this courtesy towards his fellows and refuses to use it as a law, a seasoning whereby all human relationship becomes palatable, the human soul suffers torture. Misery arises and real friendship, that springs up so easily from a basis of courtesy, becomes impossible.

The sun shines upon us all and rules this material world with its light, the light that is life. Where the sun does not penetrate we light our lamp or turn the switch, but we prefer the rays of the sun, which give us a light, a life, a "sunshine" that the electric bulb can never supply. So in the world of man it is upon the light of love that we are dependent for human sunshine, for life and joy and beauty, for the "good life". There are regions in our daily life where our touch with our fellows is so meager that this light does not penetrate, and we have to fall back upon courtesy. The tip itself, handed surreptitiously to porter or waiter, is a recognition of the fact that, however efficient the machine with which we are momentarily in contact, direct human service demands direct human recognition and so it has become the civil thing to do. We do it surreptitiously because the management has warned us that their organization and remuneration are so efficient, that it has reduced to the lowest fraction the need for human contact, that such a custom is not only unnecessary but even illegal. Such is the complication of life today that most of our money, which is the measure of our power over our fellows, "changes hands" as we say, without those hands ever coming into civil much less friendly contact. We sign cheques, we drop money into slots, and we push it through pigeon holes, where a hand but no face takes charge of it. Through our failure to light the lamp of civility, where the sunshine of friendship cannot reach, we hurt ourselves at the same time as we deprive others of their self-respect, and deny to them their own human significance.

In a loveless world, a world where men have ceased ever to be civil, a world of "foreign investment", comes Nandini, the embodiment of that light that is beauty and love. She represents the highest truth in the human world, in the nature of man, a truth for which all down the ages, the great have lived, suffered and even died. She too is willing to suffer torture, a death, a mental crucifixion. In losing her lover and her own life she loses her all to save all, the truth of love, for humanity. She offers herself for Ranjan, for love has life in its keep.

So it is that, according to the measure in which we fail to reach this relationship of love in our relations with our fellow men, our life is incomplete. We suffer, we do not deserve peace, if we cannot afford to love. And thus men organize themselves for all kinds of ends, excellent in themselves, but fail to recognize this root principle of love that is truth, of truth that is love, in their politics, their worship, their education, their business, their investments, their imperialisms. Just so long will they be capable of progress, just so long will they tread the path of inevitable destruction. Nature is never so impatient as with those who would divest her of beauty for selfish ends. Without a common love, a common appreciation of all that is good in man and in the world, it is easy for some tyrant force to find entry, to assert supremacy and to overthrow the little good that remains in a general destruction.

The problem is simple, the cure is simple, so simple that we have grown clever enough not to see it. The highest goal of all is love; a love that each of us is still able to recognize and appreciate, not an abstraction and not an organization, but a spirit, a truth for which men, in all times and countries, have been willing and eager to make the supreme sacrifice, believing that behind this spirit in man, which can be felt, almost touched, lay an objective background which they termed God. To them God was love. In this God was possible and easy for all men to find a fundamental union, which was truth. Even if we do not believe in this God, or in any God, yet our experience in home, or family, or community, or country, tells us that love is truth.

The diggers, the King, the Governor, these were men who had no love for the medium in which they worked, for the soil that they were bent upon exploiting. In their efforts they never hesitated to litter the earth with their ugly piles of rubbish in the name of progress. Yet the law of love holds good in the world of nature as well as in the world of man. It is through love for the soil, and for the cherishing of it, that the soil responds to our touch. At that touch our own hurt is healed. In mutilating the soil, that source of beauty that is also wealth, we mutilate ourselves. It was the same soil that these villagers had cherished, cultivated and loved, out of which they had grown and produced their needs of livelihood, food, clothes and implements. In it they were now digging their own damnation in service to the god of greed, of profit making, but no longer to the ideal of mutual co-operation and love.

Until Nandini came they had not realized that "the times were out of joint" or that there was any more human mode of existence. They accepted their surroundings as King, Priest, Professor and Governor ordered or taught. They took for granted the perpetual domination of the strong, the continued oppression of the weak, and that, in the effort to pile up material wealth, they should, by their own fellows, be transformed from men into machineries, to the mutilation of their own humanity.

Suddenly in the face of this vision of truth, of beauty and of love, the "perfect love which casteth out fear", they realized the greatness of their deprivation. Snatched from her village and her love to satisfy the self-indulgence of the King, to be dissected into her several component parts and analyzed, her hands, her soul, her body and her brain, each with its own marketable value, each capable of being turned to some "useful" purpose in the adding up of wealth, she defeated all by spreading an atmosphere of love wherever she went, in the study of the "dry-as-on dust" Professor, lost in his maze of facts, in the office of the file-grinding Governor, even in the room where the policemen kept their thumb-mark register and their card index catalogue. There were of course some who had by long pruning lost all sensibility to love and beauty who had developed a crookedness which could only recognize love as sentiment, and beauty, as effeminacy, who had feasted their souls upon the ugly until they had become suspicious of anything so naked as the truth. Since ugliness is a lie, as lack of civility is a lie, and is a refusal to recognize that beauty is truth as well as love, so beauty itself is invincible. Had the King failed to break the flag-staff with his own hand, it would have been merely a question of time before the very foundations of his vast structure would have been sapped and brought crashing to the ground by the invincible truth of love.

Perfection of order, of law, of government, of empire, of organization in church and state, society or commerce, this is the perfection of machinery and not the creation of happiness. Like the red oleander flower happiness too must be the fruit of love, of labour that is true, that is civil, that is honest, the fruit of human sympathy and consideration, and of human sacrifice in the cause of that great unity which is truth.

Appendix II

Tagore on Red Oleanders[2]

Some criticisms of my *Red Oleanders* that have appeared in the English papers have convinced me that to a considerable portion of my readers in England this play of mine seems obscure in meaning. Such a fact, I believe, almost always comes as a surprise to an author, because generally a work of this nature springs from a vision that is vivid to himself and a feeling that belongs to his direct experience. It is not for me to discuss the literary qualities of this book, which, being a mere translation, can have no pretension to a permanent place as literature in a language not the author's own. But I think, in justice to myself, I should make it clear that it has a definite meaning which can legitimately claim literary expression.

There was a time when, in the human world, most of our important dealings with our fellow-beings were personal dealings, and the professional element in society was never hugely disproportionate to the normal constitution of its life. Therefore, naturally, in the tradition of literature, which is the ideal expression of man's life, interaction of human relationship have so long occupied the most important position.

To-day another factor has made itself immensely evident in shaping and guiding human destiny. It is the spirit of organization, which is not social in character, but utilitarian. Christian Europe no longer depends upon Christ for her peace, but upon the league of Nations, because her peace is not disturbed by forceful individuals so much as by organised Powers. Naturally, in all organizations, variation of personality is eliminated, and the individual members, in so far as they represent the combination to which they belong, give expression to a common type and very little to their uniqueness of individuality.

But the personal man is not dead, only dominated by the organised man. The world has become the world of Jack and Giant—the Giant, who is not a gigantic man, but a multitude of men turned into a gigantic system.

I am not competent to say how Europe feels about this phenomenon produced by her science. Very likely her stout-hearted Jack is already busy making breeches in the walls of this fortress. But I can say, on behalf of inarticulate Asia, what a terrible reality for us, is the West, whose relation to ourselves is so little human. The view that we can get of her, in our mutual dealings, is that of a titanic power with an endless curiosity to analyse and know; but without sympathy to understand; with numberless arms to coerce and acquire, but no serenity of soul to realise and enjoy.

It is an organized passion of greed that is stalking abroad in the name of European civilization. I know that this does not represent the whole truth as to its character, and therefore the pity of it is all the greater when mainly this aspect of it is forcibly presented to us, causing the spread of dumb sadness over a vast portion of the world and the dread of a devastation of its future into an utterly bankrupt life. Such an objectified passion lacks the true majesty of human nature; it only assumes a terrifying bigness, its physiognomy blurred through its cover of an intricate net-work,—the scientific system. It barricades itself against all direct human touch with barriers of race pride and prestige of power. The impersonal pressure which, from its aloofness, applies to our living soul is enormous ever narrowing our prospect of growth, smothering the power of initiative in our mind.

Once our people had either an Akbar or an Aurangzeb to deal with; now we have an organised avarice,—frightfully simple in its purpose, mechanically complicated in its process. Its messengers who come to us—be they Lord Birkenhead or Lord Curzon—are never for us our fellow-beings in flesh and blood, as were Julius Caesar and Antony who could easily find their immortal places in Shakespeare's drama. They are abstractions, at once far and near, and therefore awful; they are obscure to us in the dark secrecy of their political laboratory and yet grimly concrete in their grasp upon our vitals.

Therefore it should cause no surprise to anybody if a poet, belonging to a continent swallowed by the menacing shadow of Europe, gives a prominent place among the *dramatis personae* of his play to an apparition which now so powerfully occupies the imagination of a vast world consisting of non-Western races. It is not an individual, but a doom; and therefore it should never be compared to such characters as Lady Macbeth by those who wish to find a literary precedent. I am told that science has become a principal subject for some notable poets in Europe. That is natural, for science has permeated Western life; it no longer has its own cradle in the secluded cells of the learned. In a similar manner, the hungry purpose, having science for its steed, running about unchecked, trampling our life's harvest, is not an intellectual generalization unfit for imaginative literature. It is intensely real; its hot breath is upon us; its touch is all over our shrinking soul. It is the principal hero to-day in the drama of human history; and I trust I have the right to invoke it in my own play, not in the spirit of a politician, but of a poet, possibly a lyrical poet.

I am glad to find that my critics readily acknowledge that Nandini, the heroine of the play, has definite features of an individual person. She is not an abstraction, but is pursued by an abstraction, like one tormented by a ghost. And this is the drama. Nandini is a real woman who knows that wealth and power are māyā, and that the highest expression of life is in love, which she manifests in her love for Ranjan. But love-ties are ruthlessly molested by megalomaniac ambition, while an acquisitive intellect plies its psychological curiosity, probing into the elusive mystery of love through vivisection.

I can assure my readers that I never meant to use this book as propaganda. It is a vision that has come to me in the darkest hour of dismay. I have a stronger faith in the simple personality of man than in the prolific brood of machinery that wants to crowd it . This personality—the divine essence of the infinite in the vessel of the finite—has its last treasure-house in woman's heart. Her pervading influence will some day restore the human to the desolated world of man. As in the animal world the physically meek has to-day inherited the earth, woman will one day prove that the meek in soul, through the sure power of love, will rescue this world from the dominance of the unholy spirit of rapacity. The joy of this faith has inspired me to pour all my heart into painting against the background of black shadows—the nightmare of a devil's temptation—the portrait of Nandini as the bearer of the message of reality, the saviour through death.

Appendix III

Tagore's poem 'Vijayī'

Tagore's poem 'Vijayī' (The Victorious) was published in the journal *Prabāsī* in 1918, and later included in the anthology of poems, *Pūrabī*. One can trace in it some of the ideas of the play in an embryonic form. Here is a feeble paraphrase of the poem:

> They were rushing ahead then in proud pace riding their triumphal chariots./ Impatient, infatuated, they were speeding along the blood-red dust of directionless paths./ All around them it was dark night when the hours were dragging along like some tardy sleep-walker;/ the wind had fallen, the birds were dumb.
>
> Their torches flared up to pierce the bosom of darkness/ the red lotus of fiery petals burst out in fierce

arrogance,/ the silent star in the distant sky just looked on like some spell-bound bee./ The voyagers thought this their torch was not just the mirage of a flickering moment./ They thought—this was the very flame of the lodestar;/ it will go on burning alongside the stars, deathless over the vast universe./ They thought—by means of the fierce strength of this very torch they will burn down the rampart of the fort of darkness,/ will snatch up the perennial treasures by breaking open the closed gate of darkness;/ will make the earth their own concubine.

Suddenly the bell starts ringing./ Waking up with a start they find they were blinded by stupor;/ had been dreaming alas of themselves/ as occupying the throne of Yakshapuri in the royal costume studded with million gems,/ as if they had plundered God's own creation with loud laughter of derision.

The new sun rises in the sky./ Look there, its flag flies above,/ shimmering in its fresh white splendour that crushes darkness./ The ashes of the burnt down torches seek the shelter of eternal sleep./ The realm of joy has opened doors, the sky radiates the thrill of joy—/ Oh, celebrate the victory, the victory of the earth, the victory of the sky, the victory of the light. (my translation)

Appendix IV

List of Tagore's Major Plays

(1) Musical drama—*Vālmīki Prativā; Māyār Khalā.*

(2) Verse drama—*Citrāñgadā; Bidāy-Abhiśāp; Gāndhārīr Ābedan; Satī; Narakbās; Karṇa-Kuntī Sambād; Lakṣmīr Parīkṣā.*

(3) Romantic tragedy—*Rājā O Rāṇī; Bisarjan; Mālinī.*

(4) Symbolic drama—*Prakṛtir Pratiśodh; Śāradotsav; Acalāyatan; Rājā; Dākghar; Fālguṇī; Muktadhārā; Raktakarabī (Red Oleanders); Rather Raśi; Tāser Deś; Kabir Dīkṣā.*

(5) Social plays—*Prāyaścitta; Gṛhaprabeś; Śodhbodh; Natīr Pūjā; Candālikā; Bāśarī; Muktir Upāy.*

(6) Comedy—*Godāy Galad; Baikuṇther Khātā; Cirakumār Sabhā; Hāsyakautuk; Byañgakautuk.*

(7) Seasonal plays—*Śeṣbarṣaṇ; Basanta; Nabīn; Natarāj-Ṛturañgaśālā; Śrābaṇgāthā.*

(8) Dance drama—*Citrāñgadā; Candālikā; Shyāmā; Natīr Pūjā; Śāpmocan.*

Notes

1. A talk of Tagore, transcribed by L.K. Elmherst in 1924, during the poet's visit and stay in Argentina, November-December 1924; published in *The Visva-Bharati Quarterly*, Nov. 1951-Jan. 1952, under the title '*Red Oleanders*: An Interpretation'.
2. "*Red Oleanders*: Author's Interpretation", *The Visva-Bharati Quarterly*, October 1925.

Published by
PEACOCK BOOKS
7/22, Ansari Road, Darya Ganj, New Delhi-110002
Phones : +91-11-40775252, 40775214, 23273880, 23275880
Fax : +91-11-23285873
Web : www.atlanticbooks.com
E-mail : orders@atlanticbooks.com

*Peacock Books is an imprint of
Atlantic Publishers and Distributors (P) Ltd*

First published 1925

Printed & bound in India by Atlantic Print Services